One Man's River

by Christopher Scalera

2015

> *She gave me the ability to jump in that river, to let go and to live on, in peace and clarity, to the river's end.* "

ISBN-13: 978-0692386651 (Custom Universal)
ISBN-10: 0692386653

Though much of this memoir is based on actual events in my life, the names of some characters have been changed and some composites have been made for dramatic purposes. The author hopes if any of his friends, family, or acquaintances see themselves reflected in any of the characters, that is intended to be in the most generous and affectionate light.

Front cover photo: iStock/Getty Images

I dedicate this book to my beautiful, kind, loving mother who left us much too soon. Not a day goes by when I don't feel her presence and guidance. She made me feel special, which has carried me through my entire life and made me know I could achieve anything. Thank you, Mom. I love you, miss you, and am forever grateful.

"By three methods we may learn wisdom: First, by reflection, which is noblest; Second, by imitation, which is easiest; and third by experience, which is the bitterest."
— Confucius

"There are no ordinary moments."
—Dan Millman

One Man's River

I lay across the hard cushion in the back of the boat. The sun beats down on my face. The rumble of the boat's dual outboard motors sends vibrations throughout my body.

"Your mother wishes she could be with you," Anthony says. Sunfish jump out of the water behind him, sending off glints of light. I have to shade my eyes with my hand to see him.

My mother's moving around on the deck behind him, like a shadow, puttering like she always did. "Why doesn't she tell me herself?" I ask Anthony.

"You know why," Anthony says.

Oh yeah, I think. I do know why. She's dead.

"But she's proud of you, Chris," Anthony says. "You should hear her brag. You made it out! And she has something to tell you."

"Oh, yeah? What?"

Anthony goes to answer, but just then, music starts playing. It's loud and drowns him out. "Take Me Home Tonight." No shit: Eddie Money. From the soundtrack of my youth. That song always conjures up hope and prom-

ise for a young man like myself.

And suddenly there's dancing on the boat. Girls I knew from high school, young and beautiful as ever, in their bikinis, bounce and shimmy around with the tune. They pass in front of Anthony (who's grinning at me), obscuring my view of him and Mom. I get lost in the song's refrain—"Just like Ronnie says, be my little baby"— when a girl's voice says my name.

"Chris," she says.

She must be behind me, because I feel a push on my shoulder.

"Chris," she says. "Chris. Get up..."

Anthony evaporates. The girls, the boat... all of it dissolves. I reluctantly open my eyes. "Take Me Home Tonight" is blasting from my clock radio. Man, I wish I could have stayed a little longer, on that water with those smooth bodies swaying towards me. But the dream is gone.

"Wake up, birthday boy," my wife says. Michelle stands over me, smiling. I wonder if she'd still be smiling if she knew what I've been dreaming.

Reaching over, with my eyes still shut, I go to turn off the alarm while Michelle is touching my nose, to rouse me.

6:15 a.m.

"Do I have to get up? I'm an old man, you know. I need my rest."

"Very funny. Remember, fifty years young, not old!" She holds out my morning coffee.

"You're the one who's smiling because you're not the one who's fifty."

"Oh, relax, it'll be my turn next year, and anyway, it's easier for a man. You become distinguished looking, more handsome. Women become wrinkly and gray and just plain ol' *old!* And, by the way, you don't look a day over forty. Makes me turning fifty even worse. I know my friends consider you the 'hottie' husband. While everyone else's man is going bald and getting round, you are a specimen of middle age perfection...no crisis here."

While I know all of this is a lie, I appreciate the fact that she's trying to make me feel better. I didn't know this was going to be so tough but I am not even out of bed and I feel *different* somehow.

"Here's your coffee." She hands me down my cup, and I sit up to take it. Of course, the coffee's the way I like it: black, no sugar.

"Thanks," I say. Sometimes I say "thanks" but most of the time I say nothing. This coffee in bed thing is our routine, the way she wakes me up every morning. It's our routine, except, that is, unless she's being mad at me for some reason. After 28 years anything can happen, the same routine. Sad, right? But when you've had a youth like mine—erratic, always chaotic—routine becomes your friend, your life preserver. Without its predictability, I would sink. Though, really, would it kill me to say a simple "thank you" out loud?

She leaves and I put my coffee on the nightstand. I check out what else is there: my cell phone, my TV remote, the noisy clock radio, and the pile of my "get wise fast" books. It's amazing how what accumulates at your bedside defines you. I glance at my wife's nightstand ... photos of the kids, one of the dog, and our wedding photo Next to that, a bottle of aspirin and a glass of water. What should I read into that?

I'm still under the spell of the dream. It was so real. I haven't dreamt that real since my mother died. It was about thirty years ago, just a few nights after. I dreamt that she was walking up a strange staircase, almost a spiral but squared off. I followed her and said, "Hey, Mom, wait a minute. I want to talk to you." And she turned to me and said, "Chris. Please. Get over it. Move on and do something with your life."

Now I get chills just thinking about it. Back then I was confused, angry. My parents had broken up, and by some miracle, I got to know her again, got a second chance before she died. Now I'm spiritually centered. I've lived a charmed life. And my mother's memory guided me. So what does it mean that she comes back to me now, on my fiftieth birthday?

I hear Michelle in the kitchen down the hall. I'm not one to rush to get out of bed. I love the early morning light coming through the slats in wood blinds. I installed these myself, measuring twice (maybe three times) as I recall a past business of mine. The Blind Man one of many successful businesses that I embarked on in life. "When it Comes to Window Coverings, Let the Blind Man be Your Guide." My slogan still makes me smile. My house was one of many "installs." I felt a rush of pride each time I hung a customer's window treatments. Pride...priceless. It's been my business philosophy from the start: "Never sell anything that's not good enough for your own home."

Getting out of bed and opening the blinds and getting back in bed (I know I shouldn't, but just ten more minutes...) gives me time to mentally prepare for the day. Or so I tell myself. I pull up the covers.

I wouldn't have started The Blind Man if it wasn't for my mother. When she died my sister Adele came to me and said, "This is from Mom." It was three hundred dollars. I guess you'd call it my inheritance. Three hundred bucks doesn't sound like much now, but back then, if I'd sold everything I had, I might have had five. So I went out, bought an old ratty van with it, and made myself known as The Blind Man. That $300.00 turned into thousands. That business was very successful, so successful I couldn't handle the volume. I sold it off and started something else.

Looking back keeps me humble. Looking around, I wonder how I got here. I think of something I read the night before, some self-help or spiritual book (lately, I've alternate between Tony Robbins and The Dali Lama, with others in between), trying to always make myself feel better about my existence, or at least make sense of it. I take in the room, getting satisfaction for having nice hardwood furniture my wife picked out at the Thomasville Outlet. The medium colored wood with marble tops match the wood floors and give the room a classic European feel. The white trim around the windows, doors and ceiling, makes a nice contrast. I was always a sucker for rich colors and fabrics, again chosen by my wife.

I check my cell for messages. I already got a couple of texts. My cousin Vinnie and our mutual friend George usually go out to lunch for each other's birthdays, so I have a text from both of them. This is the same crew that takes an annual Vegas trip with our wives. My wife loves this trip. It usually means a great gift for her in one of the designer boutiques in the casino, maybe a real Louis Vuitton or Gucci handbag to replace those knock-offs that she's always toting around. Funny that their texts both send me only birthday greetings, but no mention of lunch. My cousin probably called in his birthday wish, then reminded George to do so. It's always a competition to see who calls first. This year Vinnie wins.

I swing out of the bed and feel the cold hardwood floor under my bare feet. Out the window I see fresh snow has fallen. Knowing that I have to eventually go out into the cold, I shiver, wishing that I was still in the sunshine of that dream.

That dream made me a little... I don't know. Uneasy. It was great to see Anthony again. I always enjoyed our long talks. He was sort of a mentor to me, turning me on to all sorts of reading and ways of thinking. But why does he show up now, this way? And what about Mom: if it's all a dream, why didn't she come closer? Is it all just because it's my fiftieth birthday? Is it that simple? Anthony said Mom had something to tell me...?

I yawn and stretch. Time for my "get ready for work" ritual. Michelle says that I have been doing the same "step by step" routine for years; again, it's the comfort of predictability.

I place my coffee by the sink in the master bath and turn the shower knob to "hot." I use my electric shaver while I give the shower a chance to heat up. I brush my teeth and jump into the shower. To get my mind focused, I repeat my mantra: "Only good things come to me as I walk in the likeness of the Lord, while maintaining the state of bliss. I am happy, healthy, wealthy, perfect and powerful." It's a lot to say, part mantra/part prayer, but if I repeat it over and over the chatter in my head calms down. I say it while driving also. If "thought is the father of the action," as Anthony once told me, then it can't be a bad idea to have some good thoughts. For me, it's like parting the clouds to let some sunshine in or weeding the garden to discard the bad thoughts, making more room for the good ones to grow. I always try to get all the positive thoughts flowing like the hot water in my shower. I must consciously work at being positive, or the negative quickly seeps in. Again, I figure it's my tumultuous youth that caused it. When I was young, negativity was always seeping in.

My mother used to call me "CJ Sunshine." I think of that as I rinse my hair. Then I call up the dream: Mom was with me last night. Anthony said she had something to tell me. If I'd slept longer, maybe I'd have heard it.

I dry off and put on my usual outfit of blue jeans and a sweatshirt, emblazoned with my company logo. I head down the hall. My wife's on the phone. Something about her voice makes me stop. Something's odd. It's not the fact that she's on the phone (she's always on the phone), it's that she's whispering. You see, loud voices (or big mouths, to put it less delicately) are a family trait in my wife's lineage. She gets it from her father. My God, that guy can bring a house down. The whispering makes my radar immediately go up, but I push it back down, continue down the hall. I don't want anything to break my routine, to interrupt my mantra.

Passing my son Chris's room, I peek in, knowing full well that he's already out, heading to school. Still hard to believe he's a senior but easy to believe that he left his wet towel on the floor for his mother to deal with. Always looking to avoid the bull, I pick it up. I drop it off in the laundry room myself. He just dodged another bullet. He's a good kid. He's the younger of my two sons.

Then I pass my older son's room. Brandon is two years older than his brother. I knock first, never knowing if he's there or not. Out of high school and having decided not to go on to college (a decision that weighs heavily on me), he's lying in bed reading.

He looks up, "Good morning, Dad."

"Good morning, Son. Rise and shine." Our little exchanges are short and sweet but always pleasant. He'll be up and out to work shortly. Another good kid. I am blessed with two loving and respectful boys. Again, after growing up in sheer chaos, having a solid family of my own is the most important thing to me. It's my measure of a life well led.

Walking through the living room into the kitchen, I hear my wife whispering, "Gotta go. He's coming." When I come into the kitchen, she's just putting down the phone.

"Morning," I say to her.

"I was wondering if you went back to asleep," she says.

My life is a series of routines, both on a small scale and large, so as usual, I walk straight into the kitchen and take my spot at the head of the table.

Michelle turns and walks to the stove. She's got eggs and bacon—my usual breakfast—cooking away on it.

I watch my wife and think, "We've been married 28 years." Amazing. We know each other so well now. How we met: I had a house with my brother Dominic, Joey K and his brother Mike. Every night was a party; the girls came and went. It was nothing for girls to sleep over, or to find them in the living room. This one night, there was a keg in the backyard, and a band— all our friends going crazy— and I said to myself, "I gotta get up early, I got a train." I was going to acting school in the city and I had an audition the next morning. I wasn't going to drink or anything; I was going to go to bed early. So I was sitting in the living room, and this girl comes in, Michelle. She was good looking and all, a classic Italian beauty, but I wanted to be alone. She came in, sat down and I said to her, "Do me a favor, get up, and get out."

She looked me in the eye and said, "I want to hang out in here."

I just said, "No. Please. Get outta here."

So she picked up the remote and started changing the channels on the TV! I said, "Listen. I want to be alone." But she just sat there and stayed. I had to kind of admire her. Man, I thought, this girl was persistent.

She told her friend that night she was going to marry me. Why, I don't know. I didn't have a choice.

I held off six years. And then she gave me an ultimatum. I held off because I figured if your mother could leave you, anybody could, and so I never let anybody get too close.

Also, I continued to date her because even before we even went out the first time she said, "I want you to come home and meet my parents." I liked that. I figured it meant she'd be a good parent.

And she has been a good parent to the boys and a great partner to me. Times I was depressed or ready to give up, she pulled me through. She also went along with my crazy ideas. Not every woman would do that.

Michelle snaps me out of it by saying over her shoulder, "We had a meeting at the school yesterday. Christopher and me and some of his teachers and guidance counselor."

"Jesus. What now?" I say.

"The usual stuff," she says. "Fooling around in class, being a cut-up with his friends, and of course, not working up to his potential."

Chris and his potential, I think. I've heard it before. His teachers always talk about his potential as if it's some imaginary bar that he can't seem to reach, but should be able to. They make it sound like he keeps falling short of something that should be easy for him. I'm exasperated. I give him everything that he wants and all I ask in return is for him to do well in school. This, too, is the same routine, year after year of school. I'll ask him, "Damn it, Chris, why can't you just do what you're supposed to do?" He always says he'll do better and I always end up smiling at him. He's a kid that's hard to get mad at because he's a good kid, a happy kid, but my wife will say, like she does now, "Aren't you going to do something?"

"What do you want me to do, kill him?"

"Don't get so dramatic, Chris, I mean do *something*. I don't know, no car, no phone, *something!*"

"Michelle, those things will inconvenience you more than him. The kid says he's gonna do better, he'll do better. Just leave it at that and we'll see how it goes."

We always want better for our kids than we had. Chris says school just isn't for him. He never wants to disappoint me, tells me he's going to be a millionaire, which I don't doubt, I just wanted him to be a well-educated millionaire. He's smart, good-looking, respectful, motivated. Both my boys are. And I love them both to death. But when I look at them during these times, I think about my last day at school, a story that I've always kept to myself. As far as they know, I graduated from high school and went on to Community College, but that's not true. I figured I would tell them the truth when they were in college.

Brandon comes in from his room, takes a seat on the couch and, with that serious look of his says, "Dad, it's driving me crazy, I don't know what to get you for your birthday. Chris and I plan on chipping in to get you something real nice, but we're stumped."

"Nothing like waiting 'til the last minute." I break his balls, not the response he wants. "Okay, get me a Starbucks gift card."

"C'mon Dad, be serious. Something good."

"Don't stress about it, Brandon. It's just a birthday, for Christ sakes!"

A look of disappointment comes over his face. He sulks away. God, this kid is too serious. This birthday is beginning to be a hassle. I wish it would just pass, already.

Michelle puts the plate down in front of me, then checks her phone for messages. Usually she sits with me, and we talk about the day ahead. This morning she's distracted... or busy with something.

"What's going on, Michelle? I heard you whisper before, and now you're checking messages. What's up? Who were you on the phone with?"

"My secret admirer."

"Come on. I'm serious."

"Oh, just a friend from the gym. She and I are meeting there later."

"Sure hope you're not planning a surprise party."

She acts all surprised. "Who, me?"

I poke at my eggs with the fork. "You know that will freak me out. I really want fifty to be low-key, uneventful. Just us."

She smirks again, like it's ridiculous to even talk about. "Chris, I get it," she says, turning to the sink. "Would I do that to you?"

Yes, I think. But I don't say it.

I place my coffee cup in the sink and head out the door. "See ya later," I say to her back.

When we were first married, I didn't tell her I loved her. I had her at arm's length. If she told me she loved me, I'd just be walking away: "Yeah, you know..." It was just the way it was. I did love her even if I didn't say it. I tried to make sure she was happy. I wish I could say I made great calculated decisions back then, but most of my decisions were fear-based. I took the path of least fear. It's been years of pulling back the layers of the onion. And Michelle helped me to do that.

"Make sure you are home by seven. I have a special dinner planned." And there they are, the words I have been dreading. The order to be home at a certain time just screams *surprise party* to me, so much so that I feel my heart begin to race.

This is going to be a tough day, for sure.

7:00 a.m.

"Every person, all the events of your life are there because you have drawn them there. What you choose to do with them is up to you."
—Richard Bach

Like always, I stop at my mother's portrait as I head through the living room on the way out the door. The oil painting's about three by four feet, one of my prized possessions. I have it set over the mantel in the living room, placed so I see it coming and going. It makes it like she's still here. I get an especially weird feeling looking at it this morning, what with it being my fiftieth birthday, and what with the dream. That dream. It keeps giving me chills. Mom was behind Anthony in it, doing something, and she wouldn't come out to wish me happy birthday. Why? What was the dream trying to tell me? I blow a kiss to the painting. "See ya later, Mom," I say to it.

My truck's parked in our circular driveway. It's a cold

morning, with a layer of frost visible on every surface, except my windshield. My wife, after cheerfully delivering my coffee each morning, unselfishly braves the cold to start up my truck. Now, I know this is a kind gesture, one out of guilt, because she and my boys have three cars warm and snug in our garage while mine sits out in the cold. But I also know that she wants my day to start on a positive note. I don't mind parking out here. I'm proud that both sons got a car on their sixteenth birthday, and that they want to keep them nice. And, my bride, well, she deserves to park indoors.

I buckle up and shift into "drive." As I do so, my routine goes into autopilot. My truck, a year-old Toyota Tacoma, is equipped with a touch screen that shows me that my iPod is already plugged in and ready to go. I scroll to my "go to" first song of the day, "Feeling Alright" by Joe Cocker. His raspy voice and funky beat is the perfect first tune of the day, every day. I jam along, singing like I'm in the shower, belting out each word like my life depends on it, and sometimes I feel this is true. I never tire of this song. It sets me up for my day: making a living as an in home salesperson opens me up to a day filled with both complaints and compliments. Best to start out renewed and energized.

I head down my long driveway (a real bitch in snow), flanked by two matched granite pillars. I always think of my friend Joe handpicking the blocks of granite and personally overseeing this job to completion.

I go left onto my street and take another left at the stop sign. I travel down the most wonderful tree-lined street, appropriately named Wood Street. These trees, beautiful in winter with their gnarly branches reaching upwards, stretch toward the gray winter sky as if their bony fingers are searching to grab the sun out of hiding. In the summer, these mature oaks fill with lush foliage and blanket each side of the road. They make me feel that I'm cocooned in the velvety underside of their leaves. All this beauty, twenty minutes north of the city. Yup, my own paradise.

There's a part of my short ride to work that I look forward to each morning. It's easy to miss if you drive in a fog but equally hard to miss if you are an observant, spiritual kind of person, like me. As you travel up the tree-lined road, the tops of the trees get so dense they almost reach across the road, meeting in the middle. This almost completely obscures the sky. Then, there is a moment where they open up and reveal the sun, right around a bend, and you get a blast of warm sunshine in your face, blanketing the interior of your car. You see it and you feel it and if it had a sound, it would be the tune of angels singing.

And then another bend in the road and there's an old church, dating back to the 1800s. It's a small white church like a cape style house with a beautiful, tall steeple and a set of double red doors. The sight comes and goes in an instant but it is so well-choreographed that you can't help but feel like the elements were placed here deliberately, one of God's little gifts.

There is an old churchyard to the left with broken, leaning headstones placed randomly, unlike the symmetrical plan of modern cemeteries. I imagine the graves were originally dug with some order to their placement. Two hundred years later, howver, the stones have shifted around in the earth. The headstones are weathered, aged and neglected and somewhat magical as the sun hits them perfectly. In this morning light, and especially during the autumn months with oranges, yellows, and reds in the background, this scene is photo-worthy. It never fails to remind me of something that I read years ago about how embracing death liberates you to appreciate life.

I know that someday one of those stones will be mine. I silently ask God that today not be that day. And I remind myself daily, at this bend in the road, a site in my path of spiritual truth, not to cling to the trivial stuff, to let go and move forward and not to get caught up in the course of the day that lies ahead, because, if I were to die tomorrow, none of this would really matter in the big picture. Let go, fear nothing, and love everybody. We are only here for a short time.

Driving by that cemetery every morning, I think of my

mother. More so today, as I am feeling very vulnerable. When I visualize her and me just sitting and talking, I get a flood of emotions that's hard to hold back.

And that takes me back to my dream. It still nags me. So good to see Anthony again, but my mother... why was she holding back? And what did she want to tell me?

• • •

Soon I come to the deli where I stop every morning. "It's The Vinyl King!" Jilly says from behind the counter. Cute. Another joke that never goes old. "Good morning, Your Majesty!"

I return the greeting by saying my usual, "And you are a royal pain in my backside!" Jilly giggles and tends to another customer as I pick up a fresh cup of coffee. It's our routine. Jilly is the owner's daughter, maybe sixteen now. I've known her since she was a kid, I've been coming here so long. Jilly calls me The King to bust my chops, but it's nice to be a household name in my neighborhood.

People used to associate me with my first business, The Blind Man. "Hey, Blind Man!" When I wanted to sell it and start The Vinyl King, Michelle said to me, "How can you do that? Everybody knows you as The Blind Man." And I told her, "These businesses are what I do, they're not what I am." I try not to be attached to anything. Attachment and clinging is the cause of all suffering. I just want to be happy.

Usually Jilly gives me the "okay" sign with her hand, like the one on my truck. My logo shows a four fingered cartoon hand making the sign, and a king's crown around it. It looks fun and friendly. At least, that's what I want it to say.

Anthony's wife Eileen designed it. She's a hotshot graphic designer, and made the logos for both the businesses. When I was starting out, I wanted to name it all "Scalera this" and "Scalera that," "Scalera everything." "What are you selling?" Eileen asked me. And she said, "Here, let me do it. You gotta look professional." And she took it away from me and did it. Never took a dime.

I scan my Lotto ticket (another chance at hitting it big), and place the exact change on the counter, say goodbye to Jilly, and head out the door out to my truck.

As I approach the truck, my Bluetooth engages. My phone is in my pocket but I am close enough to jump in and grab the call, hands free. I didn't even spill my coffee. I hit the green button and before I have a chance to say hello I hear, "Bro!" over the speaker. It's my friend Pasquale, who is a year and one month older than me. "Getting old, big 5-0!"

I give my usual reply of "Cool Cat, where ya at?" It's something everybody expects me to say because, well, it's what I always say. I like the way it sounds. "Yeah," I say to him, "but the doctor says I'm getting healthier and better-looking with age. A medical wonder!"

"Cool Cat, your big day falls on a Friday, how lucky is that? What are your big plans?"

"Michelle keeps asking me what I want, but I don't want anything, I keep reminding her that we went big on my fortieth." That would be the family trip we took to Italy, before the recession. We had extra money and put it to good use. Who knows when I would get a chance to spend quality time like that again with my boys? We enjoyed every minute. I'm more conservative now.

Pasquale's voice snaps me back. "You still there?"

"I don't care about fifty, I'll go big on sixty. How's everything with the wife and kids?"

"Great," he says, "but running a little shy on funds. Things at the airport are slow."

Oh no, here it comes. He rents a hangar where he works on small planes. He's a talented engineer. I take a breath and reply, "Well, please don't ask me for money. Winters aren't good for my business either. No one wants exterior work done in the middle of snow."

Silence for a second, then he says, "Okay, Bro, gotta run. Just wanted to say hi." And he hangs up.

Huh? My, that was short. Usually he rambles on. Either he was feeling me out for money or he got another call. My wife probably asked him to call, to test the waters and see if I give any hint to knowing about the surprise party. That is, if there even is one.

But, some pieces are falling into place. Something's up. I'm becoming very suspicious, and my evidence is Michelle's whispering and my brother's phone call. Knowing how much it means to my wife to make every birthday special, I just know that this being my fiftieth, she must have big, loud, surprise-filled plans. While she always reminds me that taking care of a home and family are two of the most important and hardest jobs someone can have, she never forgets to show me her appreciation for being able to do just that, and not having to work outside the home. Michelle likes to call herself a "domestic engineer," but I wanted her to be home for the kids during those years when they really needed her. I realize what a huge undertaking her job has been, and while I recognize that silently and selfishly, I would never let on to her how valuable I realize it's all been. Keeps her on her toes.

I shake my head, and sip my fresh coffee. All this preoccupation with my birthday has got to end. Time to remind myself to be where my feet are, and be in the present. Everything is great when you are in the moment, not jumping ahead or falling behind in your thoughts. But it's human nature.

I think of my birthdays as a child. I can't remember too much before my parents got divorced. I was nine at the time. One or two monumental blow-ups come to mind and then it was over. The details are blurry, probably suppressed, but one day I woke up and my mother was gone, just like that—no explanation, no note. Just gone.

We at the time were five kids and we all lived with my dad. We had no choice. Looking back, I see that this all took a toll on him as well as us. But, it was a lot for a kid to digest.

My dad went off the deep end, drinking a lot. At first my older brother John and sister Adele tried to hold things together for the younger kids. But they were only thirteen and fifteen, kids themselves. We moved around, renting here and there, like gypsies. Some birthdays came and went without acknowledgement. I would never say anything. I felt better feeling bad for myself. I got real good at that.

I often wonder what it would have been like if my parents stayed together. Maybe I wouldn't have had to work so hard at finding peace, maybe I would have stayed in school, gone to college, really been somebody. Self-pity never produces good results. Before I get sucked into the pity of the past and the challenges that a slow winter puts on my present (in a business that suffers in the cold, dark winter months), I tell myself to realize that life can always be a struggle, if you let it be.

This is what I am thinking as I pull up to my office, the building I own with my partner Kevin, in the center of my town. I shift back to my positive mantra and get on with this day. Screw fifty!

My dad left a voice message, but I will call him back later. I don't like to talk on the phone during the morning routine. It throws me off.

· · ·

When I was fifteen, I was on the bus, dreading another day at another school. I was sitting next to Joey K and I turned to him and said, "I am not going, I am getting off this bus." He didn't try to stop me; he probably knew by the look on my face that nothing was going to stop me. I walked to the front of the bus. "Mr. Scalera, sit down before you get thrown off this bus!" shouted the driver. I told the driver to pull over, and he insisted again that I sit down. "Pull over or I will punch you in the back of the head," I said, and I'm sure that my determined tone convinced him to do so. He opened the door and I got off. I was about five miles from my home. That was the longest walk of my life.

When I got home, it was still early. For some reason, my father was home. I walked in the house and he said, "What are you doing home?" I tried to explain to him how I knew how to read and write (which wasn't completely true) and that I had no need for further schooling. I told him I wasn't going back.

My father very calmly told me to go upstairs and pack

my clothes, everything I owned. He was so calm, it was almost as if he had this planned for a while and was home just waiting for the day I would actually walk in with my announcement.

Everything I owned fit in a paper bag. And that was the last time I lived home, under my father's roof.

If I wasn't going to school, I would go to work. My father knew a guy who had a pig farm in the Catskills. This plan did not sit well with me. I liked the part about the free room and board but not the part where it came in exchange for hard labor on, yes, a pig farm. And there is where I stayed, many times alone, for days on end, cutting wood, taking care of the animals, and sometimes truly regretting my rash decision to get off of the school bus.

There was a barn the size of a football field with pens on both sides that housed the pigs. An alley wide enough for a truck to run up the center that gave access to both sides. Every morning I would get up around six, load the truck with bags of feed (about fifty pounds each) and drive down that center alley unloading bags, ripping them open with a spade, and filling the troughs along the way. When that was done, I would repeat the process, this time with water, cleaning out the pens along the way.

It was backbreaking, dirty, smelly, monotonous work. Initially I embraced it but quickly I saw the error of my ways. I was living on a pig farm, and I was out of options.

I was doing this routine twice a day and then I would get to eat. Boss says, "Pigs come first." How about that. God, those pigs would be squealing so loud, sometimes I still hear that sound. One good thing, I learned to drive on that old pickup.

During the months that I stayed there, I had one fun day. The boss was out working on a tractor in the field. I was stacking wood. It was a hot, sticky, humid summer day, just like every day. I could remember thinking how my friends must be sneaking into the reservoir back home for a cool swim, and here I am half dead in the sun. I hear, "The hog's out, the hog's out! Get the chain by the barn door!" A four-hundred-pound pig had escaped from the barn.

I ran to the truck, reached in for my work gloves. I then ran and grabbed the chain and threw it in the back and sped around to the back of the barn. The boss hopped in, and without missing a beat, we headed out into the field and began chasing down that hog.

It was a wild ride but it was short, considering that a four-hundred-pound hog can't outrun a truck. He finally got tired enough so the boss could jump out and get a chain around his neck to get him back to the barn. All in all it was a two-hour ordeal of fussing with that hog, with the boss yelling, "Turn right!" "Turn left!", trying to cut him off and herd him back towards the barn. It was a real riot and broke up the monotony of the place. There were a couple of times after that I thought about letting out that big, fat hog just for kicks.

We didn't talk much or see many people. I slept, ate, worked and, ironically, read. I had to do something. I was feeding pigs and cleaning up pigsties. I was cutting and stacking wood. I was nothing more than a farmhand and was having regrets.

I called my dad. "Please can I come home?"

"Sorry kid, we moved (again) into a one bedroom, I got two kids sleeping in the living room as it is. Stay there and learn a trade." Learn a trade? What fucking trade was I going to learn her? Be a pig farmer? That wasn't what I had in mind.

One night, sitting in my shack in the mountains, I decided to hit the road, no more farm life for me. I put my stuff back in a paper bag (I think it was actually the same paper bag I used to leave my father's house) and headed for the highway. I started hitchhiking my way back to civilization.

It's funny, to this day my father tells this story with pride, the story of how he made a man out of his boy by sending him away to live and work on a pig farm. He tells a glorified version, and in public I always smile and agree with him. "Yeah. Dad, you made a tough decision." Though honestly, I know his version of "the making of a man" isn't so accurate. I smile and agree; anything he says, I just agree.

7:30 a.m.

"Obstacles are necessary for success [...]
victory comes only after many struggles
and countless defeats."
—Og Mandino

From my truck, I can see that the lights in the office are on. I pull around back to park. There are no other cars in the lot. Everyone has checked in for assignments are on the road for the day. As long as my salesman and I make the sales, all is fine. It's that simple. Sell the job, do the job, collect the money, pay the bills, pay our crews, that's it, over and over. Do a great job, get the next. Screw up, get nothing. Therefore, don't screw up.

I enter through the side door instead of the showroom. I head straight for the answering machine. Two messages. The first one is a hang up; some perspective customers hate to get a machine. The second one is from a supply house.

"Windows are in, can deliver them anytime, give me a

call, and maybe I'll see you for your birthday."

No need for him to say who it is; the guy and I have been doing business since we opened up, years ago. But as I head up the stairs it occurs to me: *How does he know it's my birthday?* Although we are friendly through business, we don't necessarily celebrate our birthdays. I don't know when *his* is. Actually, without my wife reminding me, I don't know too many birthdays at all.

Our showroom is a small, freestanding building, customized to perfection. The first level is an open floor plan with a reception counter, behind which is a compact and efficient office manager set up. The counter itself is a stone façade with a granite top. Three classy glass light fixtures hang overhead along its length. Makes a great first impression. The floor is a terra cotta tile with a coordinating border. My favorite part is the mosaic inlay of our company logo. I can remember its installation well. I think I took a dozen photos. It's one of those unnecessary splurges that brings me joy every time I see it. I guess that would bump it up to a *necessary* splurge, after all.

There is a large conference table with leather swivel chairs (which is actually a great hang-out spot for friends since most sales are made in the customers' home) and sliders that lead toward a back area with a couple of desk and computer stations and file cabinets and bathroom. The walls throughout are covered in samples.

I climb the stairs to the upper level. It's a loft setup, more relaxed, with a couch and loveseat, coffee table and big screen TV. Two large windows give it a lot of sunlight. There's another bathroom up here and two offices.

My office is well lived in, though most of my work is done on the road. Still, it's filled with personal touches, photos of friends and family (including my parents' wedding photo), a stash of cigars in the back of a drawer, and of course, some inspirational materials (a copy of *The Master Key System* by Charles F. Haanel, a must for a sane mind), and go-to business "bibles" that I thumb through to refresh my skills as a salesman. Sitting at my desk gives me a sense of accomplishment. My partner Kevin's office is a bit more, shall we say, minimal. The family photos are there, one of each of his two kids and his wife, but since his entire day is spent as office manager, he pretty much lives behind the reception desk.

I met Kevin about twenty years ago. I was working for a local politician's contracting company at the time. I was honing my sales skills and I was good at it. Kevin called and wanted some interior and exterior work done on his house. He lived on a nearby lake, and needed stonework and chimney work. Their house was pristine and in an affluent but understated neighborhood. You never knew, your neighbor could be the local schoolteacher (as was Kevin's wife) or a bestselling author or artist. It's where people wanted to be for a quiet, bucolic life. Some New Yorkers just kept weekend homes there and some lived year round, like Kevin.

I went out to meet him and instantly had a good feeling about him and his wife Teresa. They were successful but not showy or braggadocios. They had a modest lake house and they wanted a high-end job. Kevin was the most organized guy that I've ever met, the opposite of me, a real pain in the ass to work for because he demanded the best, but the way they treated me and the workers was top notch, better than any job I've ever been on.

They were very generous and kind, always a cooler of cold drinks and a pot of coffee with doughnuts or cake. One day I showed up and Teresa was cutting up a watermelon while Kevin was barbequing the guys' lunch. He worked out of the house so he was always there. They definitely spoiled us. I had to tell him to stop or the guys would never want to leave. I was the foreman on the job so we met every day. I knew he'd have a six-page punch list waiting for me each morning that required me to do a breathing exercise on my ride in to prepare myself. While having coffee, we would go over it together. This guy had a system for everything, even pouring his coffee, milk and sugar first, then the coffee. No other way would do it for him. "Makes it taste better," he claimed. Who am I to argue? Everything had to be perfect and he saw that I had no problem with that. We gained tremendous respect for each other.

Kevin and I got to know each other well. We were on his job for months, and as time went on and the job got bigger, we became even closer. He said, "If you ever want to get involved with your own business, let me know. I would join you without question." Now, sometimes people say stuff like this, by way of a compliment, and don't really mean it. But this guy meant everything he said. He saw that I had it together. He knew my boss didn't appreciate my gift to sell and to make a customer so comfortable that a job would double in size, that my rapport with my men (Big Joe and Uncle Joe among them) was impeccable. My boss always wanted me to cut quality and therefore cut costs and get out of a job as quickly as possible. That's not how I like to operate, and Kevin identified with that. Needless to say, Kevin and his wife got the best job I ever did, and I felt comfortable approaching him months later with my idea for a business specializing in exterior work. I met with him and Teresa, presented my idea, put it all out there in a nice professional presentation. Not one to make a snap decision, Kevin said he'd let me know. I knew he was both impressed and intrigued, so I was ready to be patient.

Knowing Kevin might be a little hesitant, going into business with someone he didn't really know on a personal level, I invited him and his wife to a Sunday meal at Big Joe's house. Teresa was Italian (and he half Italian) so I knew this would be right up their alley. Big Joe's dad once told me, "Tell me who you hang out with and I'll tell you what you do." I wanted Kevin and his wife to see me in my element. So Sunday at Big Joe's came, and there was the usual, a big feast. Joe cooked all day: Portobello mushrooms stuffed with crabmeat, mozzarella and garden tomatoes, broccoli rabe and sausage and homemade wine (and a tour of Joe's wine cellar), different cheeses and dried sausage... the works. We set a table for twenty in the basement, and all the guys were there and the ladies, too (usually they stayed upstairs but today they were included... we didn't want Kevin's wife to think we were Neanderthals!). The basement kitchen was the guys' kitchen, and Joe was in there stirring a big pot of sauce with a two by four while he explained to Teresa how he made his own bracciole and sausage. We ate and laughed, told jokes and stories, and they fell in love with us as we all fell in love with them. It was a great day. When we said our goodbyes we promised to talk the next day. I knew he was going to do it.

So Kevin and I went in on The Vinyl King together. I needed him for his organization and business skills. And with my sales skills, and knowledge and experience in running the jobs on site, we were a match made in heaven. We've had a perfect partnership since.

• • •

Looking around at all I have and have made, I think it's a far cry from the old days. Jesus. Turning fifty makes you nostalgic.

After I got back from my time at the pig farm, I slept here and there, with friends and relatives, in cars, on couches, even in abandoned houses. I was looking for a job.

One day I walked into a small gas station, the old kind, two pumps and two bays for mechanic work. I wanted a job pumping gas; that was one skill I had.

I entered the front door of the attached convenience store and came face to face with a woman working the counter. She looked me in the eyes, and had me locked in her gaze. I got goose bumps and my hands went clammy. I couldn't find my voice, though I couldn't tell why.

She had black hair and brown eyes and an olive complexion. She was five four, much older than me. Thinking about it now, I get a rush of feeling. But despite this, she was pleasant looking, with a warmth that immediately drew me in.

"Chris." The way she said it, it wasn't a question. Just a soft spoken statement.

Though I hadn't seen her for years, and thought that she was dead, there was no mistaking that this was my mother.

"Mom," I said. There was no other reply on my mind and heart. And then, to break the tension, I gave her a big smile, and not knowing whether to shake hands or kiss her, I went in for a big hug.

My mother was always beautiful as frozen in my memory, and I'm glad I was able to get that portrait of her done, the one in my living room. She looked worn out then, seeing her after so long. Life had taken its toll, I guess. Years of anguish and heartache took on an energy and passing from her to me, and me back to her.

We talked for a while. It turned out that for the past seven years she had been living just a town away. She owned this gas station and, needless to say, she gave me a job.

When she found out that I was living in a car she let me stay with her for a couple of months. She lived in a one-bedroom cottage out behind the gas station and it had a great pull out couch. I had a chance to save up for my own apartment while we got to know each other. I laughed like a little kid and she laughed at all of my stories. We were good for each other. We didn't talk about what happened, why she just up and left. I guess I didn't want to know why. I just wanted to never let her go again. I bathed in her attention, and her sheer presence lifted me higher.

In a couple of years, she died from lung cancer. She was forty-seven years old. I blessed the day I walked into that gas station, I thanked God for a second chance at being with my mother. But inside I curse something else that put me in all of this heart wrenching mess to begin with. The worst part was suffering this tremendous loss, again.

• • •

That painting of her in my home, the one I always look at, coming and going into my house. That's a story, too.

A couple of weeks after my mother died I was helping out a friend while he worked on a home. It wasn't my job; it was this guy Bobby's. He just needed me to hand him material while he was on a ladder doing exterior work and, you know, we help each other out. It was a Friday night. The homeowner invited us inside for a cool drink and we accepted. As we walked through her living room, I noticed that an easel was set up. She was a painter, and she was doing a portrait of someone, working from a photo taped to the corner of the canvas. I admired her work and others that were hanging on the wall.

"This is beautiful work, Ma'am," I told her. "It looks just like the person."

She smiled and thanked me. "I've been doing it for awhile," she said.

"Painting?"

"Portraits. It's my specialty." She told me her name, and I looked her up later. She's famous, I found out.

"You're very talented."

"After awhile, it becomes work," she—I'll call her

Mary— said. "I'm glad it's appreciated. I've been around long enough to paint four presidents." She sighed. "Not too many people want portraits anymore. They're considered too formal. People would just as soon blow up a photo of the person. But a painting has a life of its own, don't you think? The oil paint almost breathes."

"What do you charge for something like this?" I said, knowing it was clearly out of my price range.

She asked me why. Did I want a portrait done of myself?

"No. Of my mother. She died recently at the age of forty seven and I would love a portrait of her."

Mary's eyes welled up as I said it. She was obviously no stranger to loss. She told me, "Bring me a photo, preferably a headshot, of your mom, I'll see what I can do."

"No, I could never pay you what it's worth."

"Just bring me the photo."

7:50 a.m.

"What is a friend? A single soul
dwelling in two bodies."
— Aristotle

My cell phone rings. It sounds far away. I realize I left it downstairs.

By the time I run down to retrieve it, the call goes to voicemail. No one uses a landline anymore.

I wait a few seconds for the caller to finish before I can hit playback. The voice is big, booming and one of the most familiar in my life: Big Joe.

"Cool Cat, where you at?" He uses my own greeting on me every time.

"What's up with your bad self?" I use another one of my standard greetings.

He replies, "What are you doing, Cool Cat? Still in bed?" He's always insinuating that I don't do anything. It's actually his way of telling me that I do too much. Big Joe doesn't have the strongest work ethic. He stepped into his family business. His grandfather brought the art of stone masonry over on the boat from Italy, and since then every able-bodied son had to learn the trade. Joe, well, he's the boss. No heavy lifting for him. He's actually branched out now and owns a bar and grill. He lives upstairs, where he surrounds himself with food, fun, and mayhem.

"I'm in the office. I have some plans to price. Hopefully, good work for the spring."

"Let's get together for lunch," he says. "I got twenty dollars burning a hole in my pocket."

Big Joe always wants to get together for lunch and play a few rounds of Texas Hold 'Em. It's like poker, dealing cards, making bets, busting balls. We put up twenty dollars each. By the end of the week, and after several lunches, we've had plenty of great games and usually pass that same twenty back and forth.

"OK, I'll call you when I am on my way over," I tell him. His place doesn't kick in 'til 9:30 or so, so that gives us time to hang out.

"OK, bring twenty bucks!" he says, and he hangs up.

I met Big Joe after our second move, after my parents' divorce. I must have been around twelve, and so was he. We became fast friends the first day of school. Joe loves to tell the story and people never seem to tire of hearing it, partly because it's true and mostly because of his delivery.

We have it down to a routine, finishing each other's sentences, but the main thrust is, he saved me.

Joe was the biggest kid in school and I was on the small side. One day, I was getting my lunch and heading toward a table to sit, the classic new kid in the lunchroom scene, looking around nervously while trying to be "bad ass" and indifferent to my new surroundings. I certainly wasn't accomplishing this outward look of bravado, and I was an even bigger basket case on the inside. I spotted a table with an open spot and I headed over. Some crazy-looking redheaded kid got in my face and yelled, "You can't sit there!"

I stuttered a "Thank you" (yup, I actually thanked him), and stumbled onto another table, only for the red headed psycho to follow me and do the same thing. "You can't sit there!" So I made it to another table, copping a seat directly across from Big Joe. "Red" followed me and got in my face again, only to be stopped in his tracks by Joe. "Leave him alone, get lost," Joe snarled, and the kid just walked away. Joe watched him leave, and as I looked at this big guy, this rock, I'm thinking, "You are my God." But of course, instead of verbalizing this, I gave Joe my apple. When he got up to leave, I got up to leave. When he went out to the courtyard, I went out to the courtyard. Basically, I never left his side again. I am still right there, him for me and me for him.

To this day, he treats me like family. His family treats me like family. His dad and brothers make me feel like I am their adopted son. His aunts are my aunts, uncles my uncles, and cousins, my cousins. I am rich in family because of these people. They are the ones that taught me about love and loyalty just by their example. Even though I eventually moved again, these people were mine forever. At the time, I knew it would always be that way.

One thing I learned is that family is where you find them. And when you find them, be good to them and hold them close. Finding good people, making them family...I've lived a charmed life that way.

8:45 a.m.

"Be kind whenever possible. It is always possible."
—The Dalai Lama

After my morning paperwork, I head out to my truck.

A woman's standing at the far end of our lot. She spots me when I come out. "Do you work here?" she calls out to me, a little frantically.

I don't know what to think. She's maybe in her 60s, disheveled, in dark blue, baggy sweatpants. She has on soiled white rubber boots and a blue wool winter hat. I must be staring, trying to assess the situation as she comes closer, because she repeats herself. "Do you work here? I have a big problem. Do you work here?"

I snap out of my trance. "Yes, I do. How can I help you?"

We're standing a few feet from each other. She clasps her wool coat closed. It's covered in animal hair, so much I can't help but notice. (This is a pet peeve of mine—no pun intended. I go in a lot of homes. Not everyone is like me: clean and neat and, well... clean. I hate leaving a home and feeling like I need a shower.)

"I think my house is going to burn down. There's water dripping through my kitchen light." There's sheer panic in the woman's eyes.

"Okay," I reply.

"I don't know what to do. I drive by here all the time and I see your work vans all the time. Can you help me?"

"Where do you live?"

"Only about a mile away."

I check my watch, and think about the day I have laid out. I can manage a detour. Besides, she looks pretty distraught. "I can take a look," I say. "Get in your car and I'll follow you."

"OK, but...but...I don't have any money." She barely holds back tears.

"Just relax," I tell her. "Let's not worry about that now. Let's just go take a look and see if we can figure out where that water is coming from."

I get in my truck, throw it into drive, and begin to follow her. I am thinking, "Great, here we go again."

There was a time in my life when I would have told her that I couldn't help her, knowing that the situation couldn't benefit me at all. But lately I am becoming aware of the power of good karma. Give out good energy, get back good energy. Do unto others, etc.

So I follow this dirty green Saturn, thinking, "If doing good things, looking for nothing in return, is when we receive the most, then I got a lot coming to me." But, then again, if I'm thinking I've got something owed to me, well, I'm off track again. It's getting hard to keep my head straight. I'm thinking that I've got to stop thinking.

A mile and a half later, we pull into her driveway, the uneven gravel making a crunching sound beneath my tires. I remember one of my childhood homes, the sounds of this gravel familiar there, too.

I pull up to the house. From my car I can see it's a mess, neglected and run-down. This roof has definite problems. The uneven melting of snow could be damming up the ice. The sun has been hitting the snow, but because of the blocked gutters, the melted water has backed up under the shingles and is probably causing an interior leak. This is a common problem when gutters are full, and from the look of things, clean gutters are a low priority for this woman.

I'm making my mental checklist of potential problems for the homeowner and potential revenue for myself. But one glance at the condition of the woman as she emerges from her car, distraught reminds me that this is no potential sale. This may even end up costing me money.

This has been a rough winter, and boots have been

mandatory. The snow is high. It's one of those winters where you feel like spring will never arrive. Business is slow now but the effects of this weather will reward my business in the spring. The phone will be ringing off the hook when the snow melts, I tell myself. People will want to repair any damage these past heavy snows have caused.

The woman takes me around to the back of the house, which is in bad shape too. Full of snow, covering God-knows-what. Rusty lawn furniture, turned on its side, juts up out of a mound. "Here's the back door, the one that leads to the kitchen," she says. I approach the window, cup my hands to shade the glare and peer into the kitchen. On the kitchen table sits a cat licking its paws. This freaks me out a bit on a hygiene level. Above its head I can clearly see a wet spot on the ceiling, which lines up directly with (and now I step back and look at the roof) a spot on the roof that actually looks bare. A roof boot comes out of the roof, prob-ably a vent pipe. They have a tendency to dry out and leak when they get old.

"You're not saying much. Is it bad?" she says.

"Well, I clearly see where the problem is and it's an easy fix."

"Don't you want to go inside? Go in the attic? How do you know?"

I tell her, "I've seen this a thousand times. Don't worry, I'll send my guys over here on their way home to fix it. A little silicone around the roof boot will do it. I'll have them inspect the roof while they're up there, but I can tell you now, this roof is over twenty years old and you probably need a new one."

"Oh no," she frets. Her eyes fill up again. "How much is that going to cost?"

"I don't know... I can give you an estimate," I say, but I can see that doesn't comfort her. "We can work out a payment plan, maybe?"

She chews her thumb, and looks at the roof like she's willing it to be fixed.

"I want to pay what's fair," she says. Her voice is trembling. She snuffles. "But, our situation..."

"Our?" This is the first she's mentioned somebody else.

"My husband and me."

"Where is he? Shouldn't he be included in this?"

The woman nods and starts walking to her house. I follow, and I'm glad I have my boots on as I walk through the muck.

She opens the kitchen door and stamps her feet as she walks through. I untie my boots and leave them neatly on the side. I don't like people tramping dirt through my house... I have the same respect for other people.

"Raymond?" she calls, peering into the next room. "A man's here."

"What's he want?" comes a voice. It's kind of muffled,

like somebody talking under covers.

"He's come about the roof." She tells me, "Wait here."

She goes into the room and I hear voices whisper back and forth. One sounds pissed. But after a few seconds, the woman calls to me, "You can come in."

I come around the corner, in what was probably once a nice living room. But now it's more like one in a hospital. A bed is set up against one wall. A pile of newspapers and magazines is on the coffee table. The television's on. The room is shabby but kept up okay, I guess. The air is musty, a combination of medicine and shut-in. The wall around the window under the roof is wet, the wallpaper bulging. That's the problem right there.

In the middle of the room, a guy sits in a wheelchair. The woman is swinging it around so it's not facing the TV, but me. She turns down the sound with the remote.

The guy looks all crumbled. His hair is gray and sticking up in places like he just slept on it. Blankets cover his legs and one of those white medical masks covers his nose and mouth. A tube connected to an oxygen tank runs up under the mask, to his nose, I imagine.

"So how bad is it?" he says. His eyes zero in, and I realize it's me he's talking to.

"Pretty bad," I say.

"Yeah, well..." He coughs a few times, then catches his breath." I used to be in the business, so I know what it takes."

"What business?"

"I was a contractor. Just like you."

"Oh yeah? Where?" I ask. If it's around here I should know him.

"In Maine. So I know what all that's worth."

"Yeah, it can be a lot."

"This house," he says. "It's been nothing but trouble since we moved in. One thing after another. We moved down here when my health began to fail. Be closer to the kids. And then they had to move away for work."

I look around. "Structurally it's not so bad. Someone just let the snow build up on the roof."

"I know, I know," he says. "I never would've missed it in the old days. There's only so much my wife knows to look for." The woman stands behind him, her hand on the handle of his wheelchair. She looks still about to cry. "I don't get out much." He feebly sweeps a hand to show all his medical stuff. He sort of laughs, but it's not happy. "I can't pay much," he says. "But I don't want the place falling in around our ears."

I look around, figure what it would take. Kevin will not be happy about this, but I feel I have to honor the guy. Besides, there's karma involved. I believe in karma, and if I can put good out in the world, my life will be defined by it.

I say, "Let's consider this fix on the house."

"Free?" The woman is genuinely astonished.

"Yeah," I say. "This time. I'll write it off as advertising."
I don't think they're ready to hear about karma. "Look, just
tell your friends about my company. I could use the refer-
rals."

"Thank you so much. Bless you, young man."

I can see the guy is smiling behind the mask. I look at
him and think, *There, but for the grace of God...*

I tell her the guys would measure her roof and I'd keep
the information on file if they ever decide to do a new one.
I know she'll never call, but I want to make her feel like
someone who may actually be able to afford a new roof
someday. I know what it feels like to be down on your luck.
I also know that being treated with respect in that situation
can lift you just a bit higher. We all deserve that dignity.

I leave her in her scrappy yard. She waves. She feels
good, and truly, so do I.

10:03 a.m.

"Every human is an artist.
The dream of your life is to make beautiful art."
— Miguel Ruiz

Pulling up to the office, I see Uncle Joe. He's really Big Joe's uncle, but mine too by circumstance. Actually, we all call him Uncle Joe.

He's been working for us eight years, since retiring from the family masonry business. All the brothers and nephews from Italy came here to work in the business. As a kid I worked with them. They knew I needed the money, and I knew I needed a family. Uncle Joe is now about seventy-two but is strong as an ox. He drives our dump truck from one job site to the next picking up the debris. The guys toss it in the back of the truck and he brings it to the dump. Most days he loves his job but after 4:00 pm, if he's running behind, he gets very cranky. Still it's easier than being a mason.

He's in great shape, always showing his muscles, and he's funny without even knowing it. He speaks with the thickest Italian accent, so thick that you can hardly tell he's speaking English. And he loves kids. Everyone's kids get a tray of cookies from him every holiday. He'll always ask, "Oh a boy, how-a da kids?" He begins every sentence with "Oh a boy": "Oh a boy, it's a nice day," or "Oh a boy, lotta garbage today," or "Oh a boy, I'm a hungry." And if your kids play soccer, forget about it! He always tells how he played professionally in Italy. It makes me feel sad when I see him get melancholy about the old days. But he's quick to tell you that America has been very good to him and to his sons. He's happy to have raised his family here.

Uncle Joe is a very proud man. He gets angry when Big Joe tells the story of how Uncle Joe came into America illegally. As the story goes, Uncle Joe was in his thirties. He jumped off a ship near the coast of Canada and swam to shore. The Italian mob got him over the border into the US in the trunk of a Cadillac. Supposedly the family had ties to organized crime in Italy and the oldest brother had to kill a man to get his passage into the United Sates. And then one by one, he brought over family members. He brought his entire family over. Uncle Joe says it's not true, he would never admit to it. He says he would never go back to Italy, "Even if they build a bridge."

When he first got here, he fixed horse races at the track

for a crime family. One day the horse that was supposed to win didn't, and they killed the jockey, so Uncle Joe disappeared for a couple of years. Though he says that wasn't true either. Who really knows? But it's a good story and Big Joe, much to Uncle Joe's protest, keeps telling it.

As I walk into the office, Uncle Joe is sitting at the conference table reading the paper. This is where I find him every morning. He always tells me the same thing, "I'm a teaching myself to read English."

"Oh a boy," he says as I approach. "Today is a special a day for you, happy a birthday, Chris! You can do a no a work today! I got you some nice a cookies for you and a your family. Oh a boy, you a gonna like a these!"

Those cookies again. The local bakery must love him.

I grab my cellophane-wrapped cookies, with the perfectly curled ribbon and I tell him thank you. The fact that I am on a strict gluten-free diet for health reasons completely escapes him. Try telling an Italian you can't eat wheat. He could never grasp that, just waves it off and hands me the cookies. The family will be happy.

"Uncle Joe, you didn't have to do that."

He says, "I love you like a son. You are a good a boy."

"Thank you," I reply. I am truly warmed from top to bottom. I am lucky to have this man in my life.

Charlie comes out of the back room into the main office. "Happy birthday, Boss."

"Thanks, Charlie." Yes, I guess I am the boss, but we are friends. He uses the term "Boss" as an endearment. Charlie has been with us as long as Uncle Joe. He's about twenty years younger than me. He's good people. We get a lot of mileage out of his Puerto Rican heritage and we get a lot of rice and beans, too. His wife, who is Irish and English, makes the best Puerto Rican food around. She speaks Spanish with a thicker Puerto Rican accent that the people in San Juan.

Charlie tells me that Kevin called in and suggested a birthday lunch at Carmine's. "Great," I answer, and I tell him that I am going to add a few of the guys. He says he'll take care of it. "We'll meet at twelve, Uncle Joe that means you, too."

"Oh a boy, oh a no, you young people go."

"Uncle Joe, just be there!" we both counter.

Then Charlie begins tackling Uncle Joe's workload for the day. He reviews, very slowly, the garbage stops and explains to him that all of the addresses have been programmed into the navigation system. At this, Uncle Joe shakes his head. He thinks the GPS lies sometimes. Charlie even tells him at what point in the schedule to head over to Carmine's. He is good with Uncle Joe. And, in turn, Uncle Joe loves Charlie, too. Charlie's family gets a lot of cookies.

I'm actually looking forward to lunch, birthday or no

birthday. Being with my guys is all that matters.

Heading up the stairs to my office I yell down to Charlie and Uncle Joe that I would see them later, at lunch.

Now I am thinking, if my wife is having a party for me, all these guys would be having a tremendous lunch plus plenty of food at my party later. So, why does she want me home an hour early tonight? Probably to give me time to change and freshen up before the big event. Ugh, I'm giving myself agida just thinking about this.

I need to clear my head and not think past lunch, so I pick up my cell.

First I call Big Joe, then Joey K, Coz and then Tim. All in for 1:00. The perfect gathering. Small, intimate, my guys, just what I like. I sit back and think, "Who else should I call?" I don't want to burden anyone with two events for me in one day, just in case there is a party. I decide to call my little Joey, the one sibling who hasn't moved away. He answers on the first ring. He's in for lunch and wants to bring his plumber friend, Johnny Rotten.

"No problem, Joe," I say. "And, by the way, thanks for calling me to wish me a happy birthday."

"OK, you got me there, but it's still morning, I had the whole day left to get around to it!"

"Yeah, yeah, just be at Carmine's at one," and I hang up.

My brother Joey stayed and did well, became a local cop. Likes to give tickets and break balls, real cop type. I think it's pent up frustration from his childhood. I guess we all deal differently. Joey's a little guy, very Italian, with a very Napoleon complex thing going on.

I intentionally left the day open. I mean it is "my day" and all. We have a couple of jobs running, so I drive out to the first one and check on the guys.

I make sure that things are looking good as I approach the site. I believe in curb appeal, even before the job is done. I feel that the process should look as good as possible so that potential customers get a good feeling when they drive by. I want the workers all to wear their company t-shirts, sweatshirts and/or jackets so they look professional.

This morning, the job site looks busy, but clean and organized. The guys are in full gear. Greetings all around, and I know immediately not to get in their way. They are focused and efficient and they don't need me to tell them how to do their job. Just the way I like it, and just the way they like it, too. A well-oiled machine. I check with the site boss and get a list of materials that they need so I can call it in. Everyone looks good and they all know me and know what to expect from me. I offer to do a run to Dunkin Donuts for coffee and donuts. It's well received. Nothing for me, I'm saving my appetite for Carmine's.

• • •

I like to think that I have a unique sales approach, called "The Elimination of Fear Gains Reception." It's my personal mission statement. People are always concerned about what can go wrong. I address their fears and try to eliminate them. In addressing a customer's fears, I get their full attention.

I start by saying, "Let me tell you about our company. We use only brand name products that are nationally recognized. We come to your job when we say we will, we stay every day till we are done with our intended tasks, we clean up at the end of every day, leaving your home cleaner than when we got there. We use our own dump trucks to remove debris on a daily basis, no dumpsters that can cause driveway damage."

And I continue with, "We are fully licensed and insured. All of our guys are in house and have been with us for many years. I personally take the job from start to finish, no misunderstandings, you only deal with me."

This last point gets them every time. The customer now is more relaxed and I have instilled confidence in their ability to choose us to do their work. Once we're a good fit, finding the right material and price is easy.

I've always loved sales. I'm a "born salesman," my friends and family say. My inherent nature is to be happy and make others happy. I have the instincts needed to do this job well. I don't know if I really was "born" to it, but I do know that my challenging upbringing gave me a sink-or-swim outlook. And, by God, not only am I going to swim, but I am going straight for the Olympic Gold.

• • •

Driving around, my mind wanders. I can't help but think about a trip I made to Florida. I had just rekindled my relationship with my mother, found her after so many years of missing her, and I took off. It's evident to me now just how unstable I was back then. Maybe I just couldn't handle being loved or cared for.

This makes me think of Anthony. He's been on my mind since my dream.

Anthony's a guy my mother introduced me to when I got back from my time at the pig farm. He used to come into her station all the time. He's Italian, in his 60s now, a Baby Boomer, with a full head of hair and a biker moustache. Plays drums in a band. Today, I have his first motorcycle, a '77 Triumph, in my garage. Very cool guy.

Back then, as he does now, he looked like an old rock and roller, but he's actually a very spiritual guy.

He used to come around just to talk to my mom, but he'd talk with me, too. I liked him immediately. There was something trustworthy and calm about him. He seemed so tuned into my emotional needs, and as I look back, I realize he was a kind of mentor for me.

Anthony was hip enough for me to enjoy his company and wise enough to advise and lead me in good directions without me even knowing it. He gave me books to read and would then ask me about them days later to see if I was reading them. At first I wasn't reading them, but then I chose to, simply so I didn't disappoint him. I started to get into them.

"So'd you read that book I gave you?" he's ask.

"What book?"

"The one by that Paolo Coelho guy, 'The Alchemist.' I think I'm pronouncing his name right."

"Oh," I'd say. "The 'All things are one' guy?"

"Yeah, him," Anthony would say. "Anything stick?"

I'd stare off in the distance, like I was trying to remember. Mind you, the scene was that we were sitting around a newspaper rack, customers coming and going, the ding of the gas pumps sounding off every for seconds. "Let me see," I'd say. "Oh, yeah. 'When each day is the same as the next, it's because people fail to recognize the good things that happen in their lives every day that the sun rises.' How's that?"

And Anthony would just chuckle, and toss my mom a glance. "Some kid you got here."

"I know," my mom would say.

As it turned out, I loved every book he gave me. I

learned life lessons and gained some self-awareness and confidence. I especially liked the Og Mandino books, and "Illusions" and "Jonathan Livingston Seagull," by Richard Bach and "Way of the Peaceful Warrior: A Book That Changes Lives," by Dan Millman. These guys all had a message that I was ready for, absolutely hungry for, and I devoured these books like they were my last meal. The information in these books became the cornerstones of my character, gave me the will to do more, to achieve something.

I started to hang out with Anthony on a social level. I met his wife Eileen and we became immediate friends. We ate out together once a week and I would stop by their home when I was in their area. Eileen was just like Anthony, and we would all sit and talk and philosophize about life. We really enjoyed each other's company. I always left their house feeling better than when I arrived. Being with them made me feel hopeful and capable, and back then, I was in a pretty hopeless state. Both Anthony and Eileen had rocky pasts, and their happiness and serenity became a beacon for me during a dark time.

As I round the bend and see my favorite church my phone rings. The name display reads "Anthony." There are no coincidences: that's something he once taught me.

"Hey, Anthony, I was just thinking about you."

He has a husky laugh from years of smoking and hard

living. "I wanted to wish you a happy birthday." I picture him in my mother's shop, us talking and laughing while my mother puttered around the place behind him. She chimed in sometimes, but usually just smiled, watching us enjoy ourselves. I remember those times like yesterday. That's probably why it's no surprise that he'd show up in my dream.

"Thank you, man. You sent me a card when I turned twenty-one. The card said, 'Everyone must have an end to journey towards, but in the end it's the journey that really matters. To live for some future goal is shallow. Enjoy the day.'" I recite this to him and it flows off my tongue like my mantra.

"That's right," he says, "Are you enjoying the day?"

"Absolutely! And now that I've spoken to you, I can die a happy man."

"Hey, you're not that old yet!" Anthony says. "You know you've always been my best student." We laugh and we chat a bit about Puerto Rico, where he and Eileen have a vacation home.

"Listen," I say. "I had a dream about my mother last night. And you were in it, too."

Anthony says, "Hope it was a good dream."

"Yeah, pretty much. But you told me she has something to say, but didn't get to tell me. Any idea what that was about?"

He's silent on the other end. I can just see Anthony smiling the same mysterious smile he had in the dream, thinking it over. "Well," he says eventually, "you know our souls exist on different planes of reality. You're mom's dead but she's not gone."

"Yeah, I guess," I say. "But you're not answering my question. Do you have any idea what she might have to tell me?"

Another pause, and he says, "Your mother was a very deep person. She said a lot of things. But no, I don't know what this would have been. Not for sure." He laughs. "I wasn't really there, was I?"

I laugh, too. "No. You weren't."

"We'll call you when we get back, looking forward to a nice lunch in the Bronx as soon as we land."

"You got it," I tell him.

• • •

Speaking to Anthony about the dream reminds me again of my mother's portrait, how I came into it. I feel blessed not only in friends, but in circumstance. Good luck comes to me, I don't know why. Maybe because I don't expect it, but a lot of people don't. Maybe I'm lucky in places I don't think to look for it.

Like Mary, the woman who painted portraits. She had

no reason to extend herself and her talent to me. But she did.

After she told me to bring a photo of my mother, I drove up to her house the next day just to give it to her. I didn't have many photos of my mother to choose from (our house was usually in such chaos, we didn't think to take them; happy families do that) and this was the best one I had. It was around ten in the morning. I was just going to leave it in the mailbox.

Mary saw me through her front window as I drove up and waved me in. We sat and had coffee.

She told me about herself, and her own loss. Mary said she was always "daddy's little girl" but that the Lord had taken her father at a young age. She showed me a big portrait she did of him. She was able to convey so much more than his good looks in that painting...it spoke of his loving, nurturing way, his kind and generous spirit. She had a real gift for capturing more than just a face.

She looked at my mom's photo. "She was beautiful," Mary said.

"Yes, she was," I replied, and felt a rush of emotion. The photo was taken in her youth, when she was about 26. Her hair was black, her complexion olive; a classic Italian beauty. Big eyes and moist, healthy lips. She was smiling and her whole life was set out before her.

Mary asked me questions about my mom, really inquired as to what she was like. I enjoyed describing her in great detail, something I never before had a reason to do. Mary held my hand gently and said she'd call when it was ready. I said no more and left.

Mary called two weeks later and invited me over. Over coffee she presented me with the portrait of my mother.

I was speechless. My mother was alive in that painting, all her nuances captured. My eyes welled up, but I knew I couldn't pay for such a great gift.

Mary read my mind and said that this was something she wanted me to have. "It's really was more for me than for you. This is a true gift and you must accept it and give it a loving home."

We talked some more, and I learned a lot about this generous woman, about her life, her loves and her losses, and I left with my extraordinary gift. I can't pass this portrait in my house without remembering my mother and the entire experience that brought her lifelike image to me, to my home. Good things come to good people. I am a good person. I received this tremendous gift.

11:14 a.m.

"The simple things are also the most extraordinary things, and only the wise can see them."
—Paulo Coelho

My cell phone rings again and I like what I see. Joey K is on the line.

"Cool Cat, what's up?" I greet him with the usual.

"Joey K looking to have a little lunch." He always refers to himself in third person, as "Joey K." It's his trademark, and it never gets old. It's how I'd identify him from an imposter, if the occasion ever arose. Though, truth be told, this guy is such an original, no one could ever imitate him. Totally authentic, the real deal. Tough exterior, but a big heart inside. That's how he manages to hold on to a lovely wife and four kids. He's a real family man and does a great job at it. I get a kick out of everything about him.

I met Joey K when I was about 15. I had just moved to another town, which meant another school, which meant moving away from Big Joe. We moved into an old, very dilapidated country house my dad rented. He must have gotten a great deal because this house was in bad shape. And we, as a family, were no better. We definitely looked dilapidated ourselves. But we presented as proud.

I figured I would take my broken down bicycle, made up of spare parts, for a ride around my new neighborhood. About a quarter mile into my ride, up a slight incline of a hill, I spied three kids hanging out. My radar went up and I immediately assumed "fight or flight" mode, not knowing what to expect. With my practiced survival skills, I assessed the situation from a short distance. Two tough-looking Hispanic kids about my age and a third happy-go-lucky-looking Italian kid. One of the tough guys was Joey K. (Jump to the future, Joey K becomes a Middle Weight Golden Gloves and pro boxer. I could have predicted this in my first glance.) Nervously, I rode up to them and gave my toughest "Hi."

"I just moved in down the street," I said.

"What's your name?" Joey K asked me.

"They call me Poison," I replied. Oh God, I thought. Did I really just say that? I made took that name up to sound tough.

He glared at me a long time with something like murder in his eyes. Then he laughed—thank God he laughed. His voice was deep, and he was 'way past puberty and well into manhood. Then his face broke into a smile. "No one calls you Poison!" he exclaimed.

My tough-guy image collapsed. And we became instant friends. We're like brothers to this day, 35 years later. Joey K loves to tell people how we met and how I claimed my nickname was "Poison." But the best part of the story is, one night a few years later, we were in a disco. A guy starts yelling to me, "Hey, Poison," and Joey K hears this. He turns to me, his eyes wide, and buckles over into a belly laugh. "Yup, Poison, that's you!" he said between guffaws. I mean, the nickname never really stuck and carried very little weight, but it was the image I tried so hard to project during some rough teenage years.

I have always felt fortunate to have Joey K as a friend. Better to be his friend than his enemy, I can assure you that. And I always felt confident standing slightly behind him when things got sticky (those disco nights could get rowdy) because, as I said on a many an occasion back then, "If you wanna piece of me, you gotta get through Joey K first!" Worked like a charm every time. Still does.

Into my phone I say, "Cool Cat, I am heading to Big Joe's if you want to meet us at the bar. Though, you'll need to sit for a few hands of poker!"

"No, I don't have that kind of time." Joey's a contractor himself. "Just a quick bite, but I'll call you later. I definitely want to take you out for your Big 5-0."

"OK, sounds like a plan. Whenever you want, let me know."

I park my truck in back of Big Joe's bar, out of sight from the street. It's bad business for my logo to be too conspicuous here at this time of day. Potential customers could assume the company owner is having a liquid lunch at some secluded bar. Not only that, but "La Fronterra" is not the kind of place where my company truck should be seen. Joe's place is popular among men, and men only, and can have a rowdy reputation.

I head in through the kitchen door and see Joe in his usual seat, a high back barstool pulled forward towards the stainless steel kitchen prep table. We much prefer casual lunches in the kitchen. His cigar is lit and he's sipping his espresso, probably number four of the day. The sturdy stool looks delicate under his almost four-hundred-pound frame. He's got on his usual uniform of black sweatpants and black slip-on shoes. You can always tell what he's been eating by the stains on his white tee. The collar is slit to accommodate his neck. His mother once said that when he was five years old, she caught him putting meatballs in his pocket. This would not surprise you. This boy loves to eat. He doesn't eat just anything, he eats the best...all quantity, yes, but all quality, as well.

Joe has pretty much just gotten up from working late. His usual crowd begins to file in at about 2:00 a.m.: waiters and busboys from local restaurants who get off work late and are looking for some entertainment, some female companionship, and plenty of booze. It's a crazy lifestyle for Big Joe, but it's more than paying the bills. With his usual business of construction and masonry being slow, this bar has proven to be a great investment, that is, if the hours and lifestyle don't burn him out. However, this kind of business usually comes with a lot of trouble. Surprisingly, the guys are very well behaved. It's usually the girls that end up in a brawl. When that happens, security throws them out and the sheriff picks them up outside and hauls them off to jail. Ironically, they then call Joe to bail them out. Who else? He lets them cool off until the following afternoon and then goes in for the rescue. Lessons learned, and the whole crazy cycle starts over again that night.

After the usual greetings ("Cool Cat" this and "Cool Cat" that), I look at the table and see that there're four sets of chips instead of two. "Who's playing, Cool Cat?"

Joe grins. "I gotta surprise for ya."

Ugh, I hate surprises.

A rustle comes from the bar area and into the kitchen walks Tim, my very first best friend ever, who moved to California years ago.

"Timbo! What the hell are you doing here??"

"Came here to see you, Pal. Turning fifty, shit, how can that be?"

"Since when do you remember my birthday?"

"Since this prick called me and guilted me into a quick trip out here." He turns to Big Joe. "I'd like to see you get your ass on a plane for a 'quick trip' to the west coast, you bum!"

Laughs all around, and I am truly touched at the visit. Though, I must admit, I am getting more dubious by the minute. Timbo wouldn't fly out here without a good reason.

I met Tim when my parents first split and we moved to the next town. I was nine or ten. Up until then, I knew only one house, one school and one set of friends. My older brother Dominic helped me through this move and would bike ride with me into town where a bunch of kids would hang out. Tim was among them. We spent a lot of time together, Tim and I, all those long summer months, riding bikes and exploring. We got along great, became blood brothers, shared secrets and petty thefts and bumps, bruises, and boyhood bragging about "babes."

Tim comes from a successful and educated family. He always seemed smarter than most and was a little guy, but with big words. Still, Tim quickly became part of our crazy bunch. As years went by and we changed schools, etc., I always made sure that with each new friendship that I made, Tim and I were together, a package deal.

"Timbo, man, it's great to see you. Wish you never moved so we could spend more time together. God, these years are going so fast." I am rambling but I seem to be a little off today from too much reminiscing.

Tim says, "I'm taking my mom's car for a spin later. I passed by that piece of shit your father rented, and I thought about that time I was supposed to sleep over your house." Oh, God, he's talking about when we were twelve. "Remember, we were walking up your driveway and that drunken Step Monster of yours was throwing all the dishes, pots, pans, even the silverware out the second story window." The broken glass was imbedded in the front yard forever after that, a constant reminder of her crazy ways. "Somebody must have left some dirty dishes in the sink and she friggin' freaked out!"

"Yeah, I remember, we ate off of paper plates forever after that episode. You were too afraid to sleep over, not that I blame you. I didn't even want to sleep there after that."

Some crazy shit went on at my house after my mother left. My father remarried and my new stepmother was there only for my dad and the booze, not for us kids. She resented that we were in the picture.

"Sorry, Timbo. I guess my house was always an education on how the other half lived."

"Hey, pal, at least your house prepared me for the real world, not like my life in La-La Land."

My house was one crazy scene. Not just with my stepmother, either. One time my sister Adele threw a knife at me at the dinner table because I called her a dropout. My sister had to leave school to help support the family. When she was fourteen she took a job at a local pizza parlor. It had its perks, like lots of free pizza for the family. We used to run a scam on the place. My sister told us to call in and order a large pie just before closing. When no one would come to pick it up, the owner would let her bring it home. We pulled this trick as often as possible. It's my guess the owner caught on eventually, but he probably went along with it out of sympathy for us. Good thing he did; some nights that was our only way to get a real meal. The moral of that story is, as the knife went sailing by me and stuck in the wall behind me, I was much more careful about the way I spoke to my sister after that. My father had to declare a rule about no throwing knives at the dinner table. I ask you, is that normal?

Timbo's friendship has meant a lot to me. He stuck it out through a lot of craziness. Timmy gave me the warmest winter coat I ever had. He literally gave me the coat off his back, and the sneakers off his feet, too. He had these sneakers that I always wanted. They were the "in" pair at the time. He had been wearing them for a while, but for me, they were as good as new. Boy, was his mother pissed. But he didn't care. He wouldn't take them back. I wore those sneakers 'til they fell apart at the seams. I was good to him too, but in other ways. It was a tough life, but we learned how to survive.

Okay, there are four sets of chips. I'm thinking, who else besides Tim?

And in walks Cosmo. Cosmo is one of Joe's brothers, one year younger.

I say, "Coz, you too?"

"I left work early to get in on this lunch and game. I hate when you guys are partying while I am slaving away!" Cosmo is smaller version of Joe. He's super nice and a real gentleman. Another family man, Cosmo lives with his wife and kids in a big house not too far from the bar. Cosmo is a generous guy. He'd give you the shirt off his back, and his shoes if you needed those, too.

"Yeah," says Big Joe, punching his brother on the arm. "Like it's a big deal to get here. You only live a few blocks away!"

"Yeah, I could hear your loud mouth from my office!"

More laughs, and back slapping. All the ball-busting makes me feel good, amongst friends, but I can't fight the suspicion: I'm more convinced than ever that a party— a party I don't want — is in the works.

1:06 p.m.

"The gem cannot be polished without friction,
nor man perfected without trials."
—Confucius

Carmine has his back to me as I enter. He's feeding an-other piece of wood into his brick oven. He's running through his lunch crowd but his mind is on us, my birthday lunch. No walk-ins yet, so he's smoking a cigar and has the exhaust fan way up.

Carmine's restaurant is very old school, with paper placemats (the kind that leave a translucent water ring from your sweaty *agua con gasse*) depicting the map of Italy. The map is hand drawn, overemphasizing the boot shape of Italy.

My friendship with Carmine developed over the past few years. He's actually from Italy, and I am mesmerized by his accent and his stories about the old country. Plus we share philosophies on life, our loves, our interests and our culture. He calls me during his slow time, between the lunch and dinner crowds, to see if I am free to come, hang out, and have a cigar and espresso, or perhaps a nice grilled chicken with broccoli rabe.

We can sit for hours, but not today.

As soon as I walk in, he calls, *"Ciao Bello!"* (if you are a guy he calls you *"Bello"* and a woman *"Bella"*), "Where have you been?" He's sitting, legs crossed cigar in one hand and red wine in the other.

"Bello, you hungry?"

In nice weather we sit outside on the patio, but today, cold and damp, we sit in a small private dining room, with a big screen TV, tables covered in red cloths, each already set with a bottle of Pellegrino. Bordering the ceiling is a wooden shelf with bottles of wine and there is a small service bar in one corner.

He gets up and makes me my espresso, My favorite thing in the room is the espresso machine, a beautiful brass work of art topped with a brass eagle. Carmine uses the finest of coffee, and takes a lot of pride in its presentation, just the right amount in a small cup with a beautiful head of perfect *crema* on top.

He brings me that plus a wine glass for some Pellegrino, no ice. (The Dali Lama always says, "All illness is traced back to things too hot or too cold." I try to stick to room temperature whenever possible). He sets the coffee before me, and exclaims, "Oh boy, look at that, beautiful!" like it's the first one he ever made.

I ask him, "Cool Cat, did my wife call you about me turning fifty, about a party?"

"No, *Bello,* but if that is the plan, you make sure I know about it."

"Actually, my friend, if there is a party, *I* will be the *last* one to know about it. So, where you puttin' us all today?"

"I wanted to talk food, see what you got planned for us today. I probably should have stopped eating two days ago to get ready!" I tease him because he always feeds me too much.

"*Bello,* you're talkin' to me. It's your birthday, private room, where else can we eat, drink, smoke, and laugh? I got you all set! It's a beautiful thing, your birthday. I got my girls running the show in here so I can relax and enjoy with you!" Music to my ears, but I know he won't sit for long, he'll be running back and forth serving us like kings, making sure everything is perfectly prepared.

"You are too good to me," I say.

"How many guys we got today?"

"We have Kevin, Charlie, Uncle Joe, Big Joe, Timmy's in town, Joey K, and of course, my younger brother Joey (not one to miss a free meal he sometimes orders two just to get the most out of it!) And Johnny Rotten. Plus you and me, that makes ten." Wow, my crew, all my boys, I get a weird feeling for a moment, something emotional runs through me, but then it's gone. Fleeting but very palpable. Strange.

Carmine sends Pedro upstairs to set up for ten while we sit and sip our espresso. The guys start rolling in. My brother first, in his patrol car, uniform a perfect fit, shoulders back, hair high and tight, he looks like a Marine. His gun is strapped to his hip. Shit, he was born for this stuff. Joey's got a look on his face that says, "Just give me a reason to shoot you," but he cracks a smile as he walks in.

He hugs me hard so I know his strength.

"Why's Johnny coming?" I ask.

"He's doing some plumbing at my house, figured I'd pay him with a free lunch."

"Oh no, Joe, it's my birthday, so you're paying."

"Not on my salary. You got rich friends, let them handle it. And warn them, I'm hungry!" Class act, my brother Joe. Same way he's always been, the "the worlds owes me" attitude.

"Joe, take it easy. Why you always look so serious, it's lunch time, relax." Carmine gets another smile out of him and we hug again.

As Joe releases me, Joey K walks in and says, "Typical cop behavior... always wants shit for free," and so the digs begin, before everyone is even in the door. We head upstairs.

Uncle Joe comes in straight from the garbage detail with Charlie's directions still in his hand. Big Joe comes in with a box of Cubans for me from everyone. He told the guys he'd handle the gift and they could pay him (you know he's tacked on a hefty finder's fee for himself). Timmy's fresh from his mother's house and needs a drink, and Charlie (thank God someone reliable was out there checking on our work) enters with a respectable "Hi, Boss" greeting with a handshake and a hug. Even Johnny Rotten gives me a big birthday greeting. He looks hungry. When Kevin enters, my brother Joey jumps up.

"Touch me, touch me!" he yells. "I never met a guy with better luck and I want some of it. I can't understand how this guy got a gorgeous, rich wife, big house, money, and cars. God, rub against me, please!" and he proceeds to pantomime a rude gesture and so the jokes begin.

I look at the table as it fills in and that feeling rises up again, but I push it down. The noise and smoke are already overwhelming and the antipasto is coming in on platters carried by a smiling and proud Carmine, my friend.

We all dive in like it's our last meal. Initially, barely a word is spoken except for the *ooohs* and *aaahs* of a bunch of *"gavones"* shoveling food into their mouths. We enjoy every morsel, every deliciously thin sliced piece of prosciutto and genoa salami, every creamy, salty slice of fresh homemade mozzarella and carefully roasted red peppers, every briny Sicilian olive and brick oven charred baby artichoke and grilled vegetables. The extra virgin olive oil is delicately drizzled over every selection and the calamari is gently fried with an accompaniment of homemade marinara. Carmine really outdid himself with the *spedini alla Romana* and the grilled asparagus with four cheeses on top. Each leaf of basil and sprig of rosemary comes from clay pots that sit outside the kitchen door. There are also pizza pies, made rustically, with everything from grilled chicken to shrimp *scampi*.

Needless to say, when Carmine stands before us asking, "Okay, boys, what do you feel like having for lunch?" we all groan and laugh and trust him to take care of us like he would the Pope. And he does.

We're in less of a rush to eat when the entrée platters showed up for a family style lunch. And so the stories begin.

Over *chicken scarpariello*, off the bone with white wine and garlic and potatoes and *seafood fra diavolo*, "hot like the devil," and *bistecca di fiorentino*, grilled steak in the style of Florence, my brother, of course, wants to know, "Who's paying for all of this?" Because if everyone is paying for their own, then Carmine better bring him a house salad. Strains of "Typical!" and "Cheapskate!" filled the room. Once Kevin says we're putting it on the company card, Joey jumps into the steak with a flourish. Carmine, adding to the joke brings out a platter of lamb chops "for Joey the cop," he says, and this pleases Joey, who really thinks the whole platter is for him.

"Hey, pass some of those down here to the birthday boy," Charlie says as he reaches for the platter and serves himself. More laughs from around the table and more stories told. This feast goes on for two hours and everyone is quite sated in the end.

This lunch has the distinct feeling of a Roman food orgy. We sit as if we have no jobs, no responsibilities, like time is standing still. It's one time that I feel like we are all truly right in the moment, not lamenting over the past, not anxious about the future, just truly right here, right now. It's very rare.

I am awakened from my thoughts by the very off key and halfhearted rendition of "Happy Birthday" that is being sung while Pepe carries in a tray of *tiramisu, ricotta* cheesecake, *cannolis,* and *pinoli* cookies. There's a sparkler fizzling away.

I am overcome with emotion. I can't say it's joy and I know it's not sadness. It's just an overwhelming feeling of fullness, of very bittersweet completion.

I stand up and gratefully thank the guys. I acknowledge my gratitude for Timmy flying in and, not one to end something without a laugh, I add, "And Johnny, I hope you enjoyed your meal but start charging my brother for your time. Don't let him bullshit you—he has more money than all of us!"

And with that, we clink espresso cups and open up the box of cigars.

As I pass around the cigars, Kevin says he's going to head off. He doesn't like the smoke, and he's said he's had enough of all of us, already. Truth is, he'd rather be in the office. Charlie heads out to a sales call and my brother heads out too, to fill his ticket quota for the month.

My cell phone rings and it's Michelle. "Birthday boy, how's it going? I hope you didn't eat a big lunch, tonight I am making a special birthday dinner."

"Don't worry, I always have room for your cooking," I reply to my bride, but I have one hand holding the phone and the other holding my stomach. Shit, I definitely over-did it. But hanging with my guys is definitely worth it. I'll have to choke my dinner down with a smile on my face, that's for sure. That is, if it really is just a family dinner, and not a party. "I'll be home at seven on the button, just like I said, don't worry."

And I hang up and let out a huge groan and pray I make it through another meal.

Carmine joins us and I give him a cigar. I begin telling my usual childhood stories, the ones that involved all of these guys so they join in and laugh like it's the first time these stories have been told.

Timmy says, "Hey, did Carmine ever hear the story about how you took off for Florida in that custom van?"

"Custom van? I highly doubt that," adds Carmine. He knows how tight times were for me back then.

Big Joe says, "Not that story again," but Joey K yells, "Yeah, tell that one, it's a good one." He's in no rush at all today.

• • •

I was about seventeen. I had a car that I decide to trade in for a van. As luck would have it, I was able to trade in for this custom Ford van with seats in the back that turn into a bed. It had a sink and a small refrigerator. It was basically an apartment on wheels for a seventeen year old, so I said to Joey K, "Let's go to Florida, it will be fun, a crazy road trip."

Joey K saw this as the harebrained scheme that it was, and said, "No way, I want to finish school."

"C'mon, we'll go see my brother Dom in Mayport, where the naval ships come in."

"Sorry, brother, you're on your own."

I begged him, but he wasn't budging. I was scared as hell to do this alone but I was determined to go.

I had no idea even how to get there. At the time, I was

working for my brother-in-law Marty at an auto body shop. I was just a helper but I managed to make a little money. I drove over there and told him that I was quitting work. I told him that my plan was to go to Florida.

"Are you crazy? Did you tell your sister?"

"You tell her, I'm leaving. Help me out, how do I get there?"

So there I was heading south on I-95 with two gallons of water, peanut butter, jelly, and bread. I'd say it was well planned out. I drove 'til I couldn't keep my eyes open, slept at a rest stop, and drove some more.

By Jacksonville I was out of gas and out of money. I pulled over at a gas station, looked over an embankment, and saw a shopping plaza down below that had a fast food joint.

I decided to walk in and ask for a job. I actually landed one on the night shift. You didn't need too many qualifications, apparently. I would start that night. So I grabbed a free meal and then walked back up the hill to retrieve my van. I parked it in the restaurant lot and waited for my shift to begin.

Close to 6:00, a crazy looking, longhaired southern boy banged on the van door to let me know he's got to train me. He asks me about my New York, plates so I tell him my story, ending with how I ran out of money and was low on luck, so here I am. He calls me a crazy son of a bitch, slaps me on the back and welcomes me aboard.

Crazy Dave was his name and he was well known in those parts. After our shift he said I could stay with his mom and him in their nearby trailer. "But first, let's fill up that gas tank, grab some beers, and I'll show you around."

Our first (and only) stop was the ocean, a spot where everyone knew Crazy Dave and where the topless dancers would come when they got off work. "Easy pickins'," is what he said, and he was right. I made friends with the girls because... any friend of Dave's... well, you know the rest.

This worked out so well that I actually ended up moving in with the girls (a better deal than Dave and his mother). The girls had an apartment they all shared near the beach. It was definitely good times for a young guy trying to find himself. Or so I thought. Actually, I ended up getting more lost than I was already. What is it that Buddha says? "You must lose your mind to find it." Well, that was definitely my process. I had really lost my mind.

Life went on like this for months. I was beginning to feel a bit homesick. I had this incredible need to see family. I was young and this good time was wearing me down, making me lonelier, even though I was surrounded by new friends. The thing about my friends was that, up until this point, they came with parents and siblings and homes and food. These new friends had none of those things. These were fly-by-night folks with no families, living in flop houses. They weren't filling the void in my life, they were just making the hole bigger.

So one particular night, after a few too many drinks, I jumped in my van and headed south. Of course I had my usual paper bag of belongings and barely said goodbye and gave no explanations. My life began to feel like it was "a story better told, than lived." Which makes sense since my life is a stream of one story after another. I was determined to find my friend Pasquale. I needed a connection.

"Wait a minute, you got all these girls and you leave?" Carmine's dumbstruck.

"Let me finish the story."

"It gets better," Timmy adds. He's heard it before.

I continue. I found my friend on his naval base. His ship was in port and he was sleeping on base while my van and I were shacked up at "a friend of a friend's" right outside the naval yard. I was sleeping in my van. Those fold down seats had become a necessity to me. This "friend" was a 24-hour-a-day drunk who was charging me fifty dollars a week for the use of his shower. I will never forget the smell of that water: rotten eggs. To this day that sulfurous smell brings me right back. There's nothing like no lather and having to hold your breath while showering to sober you up a bit.

Sadly enough, I was beginning to fit right in. This guy had drunks and drug addicts in and out of the shack all day. I was ten pounds underweight by now and things were starting to go from bad to worse.

One night, the Marine boys from the base headed into town for the drugstore. They would buy up all the Robitussin DM cough syrup because it contained an ingredient that could get you high. This stuff would really mess you up.

Five of the Marines and my friend downed a bottle each and chased it with a couple of beers. They were totally tripping and had no money to crank their party up to the next level.

One genius decided that it would be a great idea to take my van and hold up a liquor store. Yup, that's right, hold up a liquor store. And they wanted me to be the driver. Now, I'm thinking, "This is a bad idea, but who am I to argue with six very large, very high military men?" But I got my guts up and said, "No way, I'm out." I feared for my life, but they basically pushed me aside and started getting crazy. My friend agreed to drive and those insane fuckers took off in my van.

I never saw my van again. Or my friend for a very, very long time after that. They got busted and my van was impounded. I took a cab to the airport and headed back north. Next thing I knew, my sister was slapping me in the face. I was asleep on a bench outside of JFK.

"You look like a bum. I've been looking for you everywhere."

"Sorry, Adele. I called you and then fell asleep." It was

me and my paper bag again, starting all over.

Back to sleeping on my mom's couch, saving up for an apartment, old job back at the service station, no diploma, hanging back with my true friends. But boy, I did come home with a lot of good stories. We told them over and over, night after night, it was like I was a cowboy home from a cross country cattle drive. My mom ended up lending me money to buy a cheap car, and life went on.

I tell Carmine more about the wild stuff that happened, he only wants to hear about the girls. I don't tell him about the longing and emptiness. That's a downer and I want to keep him entertained. But I think anyone could see right through it.

• • •

It's time to head home to my big surprise. I don't feel bad breaking up this get together because I know that within a few short hours we'll all be together again at my party. And we'll be telling the same stories and smoking the same cigars. I decide to feel the guys out.

"C'mon, spare me the misery. Does my wife have some kind of party planned for me? Just tell me."

"You know, you said 'no big deal' about this birthday, so nothing is planned. This is it, my friend." Replies like that from all. I search their faces and I actually believe them. I can't tell if I am relieved or disappointed, but either way, I get hugs all around and we all go our separate ways.

I pull Carmine aside, thank him for the lunch and for being so generous. Before Kevin left he paid the bill. Later he tells me that Carmine charged us ten dollars a head. Christ, that wouldn't have even covered the Pellegrino! What a guy, the best. I am rich in friends. We thanked each other for our friendship.

Tim's heading to see his mom—"Guys, don't tell her that I stopped here first!"—and Coz has to bring his son to baseball. Joe and I finish our cigars and discuss our next meal. When most men are discussing big breasts and short skirts, Joe and I discuss chicken breasts and skirt steak sandwiches. OK, truth be told, we discussed other things too, I may be fifty, but I'm not dead. Oh. God, though I will be if I don't hightail it out of here and get home to my family dinner. I better muster up some kind of appetite as well since Michelle and I are big on having a family dinner each night.

5:45 p.m.

"Our greatest glory is not in never falling,
but in rising every time we fall."
—Confucius

I head back to the office to check my messages. My stomach churns. Oh, man, I'm thinking. I overdid it after all. How dumb of me to eat and drink all that, when I suspect Michelle has something ready for me back home. Okay, I'm bloated. You're only fifty once, right?

My phone rings. The display reads "POP'S CELL." Shit, I forgot to call him back.

"Hey, Dad."

"Son, have you forgot that you owe me a barbeque?"

Not the greeting I was expecting, but typical. He's always asking me for something.

"Today's my birthday," I remind him before this gets any more embarrassing. "What do you have for me?" My dad lives in a trailer park down in Florida. I know I am not getting much from him. He barely makes ends meet without my help.

"I thought your birthday was tomorrow," he says. "I was gonna call you tomorrow."

"Nice try, Dad. Hey, now you don't have to. Just say 'happy birthday' now."

A couple of months ago I was down south visiting my dad. I went with a good friend Sisto, who is Big Joe's cousin. I'm godfather to his youngest son, a great honor that I don't take lightly. Sisto lives on the west coast of Florida and my dad's on the east coast, so when I go down, I take the opportunity to kill two proverbial birds with one stone and visit them both.

I flew into the west coast and checked in with Sisto and his family, and then I drove east. Sisto went with me.

My father had found a guy with a used barbeque for twenty bucks. He gave me directions and sent us over to buy it, driving my father's neighbor's rickety old pickup. Dad stayed home and started marinating the meat.

After about a half hour, we arrived at a junkyard of a house, a real falling-down shack. In back was a rattling old barbeque right out back next to the woodpile, paint peeling, held together by rust. With one wheel missing and bent grill rack, this Weber had seen better days. But it looked exactly like a piece of shit that my father would send me thirty miles away in a busted old pickup to retrieve for twenty dollars.

"Hey, you John's son?" an old guy called out to me. He had ponytailed gray hair, dirty cutoff shorts, stained tee and stained teeth, flip flops, the whole nine yards.

"Yup, that's me. I am here for the barbeque. That it?" I pointed to the wreck of a grill.

"That's it. Seen many a good piece of meat." I instantly lost my appetite. "Let me help you load it up, but you got my thirty bucks?"

"Easy, big fella. The deal was twenty. He didn't pay you up front?"

"Oh, yeah, right, twenty. I forgot, I cut him a break. He's the best, your dad. No, he said you'd pay me."

"Yup," I said, rolling my eyes. Typical that he'd set me up to pay. "He's the best."

The three of us (really, just Sisto and I) loaded the grill on the back of the truck. I handed the guy a twenty—my twenty, mind you, not my dad's.

The barbeque slid around the bed of the truck as we headed back to the interstate. Sisto kept saying we should pull over and secure it.

"Just reach through the window and hold it towards the cab, I'll go slowly." I told him. It was probably one of the worst plans in history. But then again, did it really matter? This piece of shit wouldn't work anyway.

We started talking and listening to the radio and

pretty much forgot about the barbeque. I pulled up to the tollbooth. I stopped, paid the attendant and hit the gas. You know that lurch forward that usually comes when you hit an unfamiliar gas pedal? Well, that barbeque slid back, hit the tailgate, flew over the top of it and landed with a crash right in the middle of my toll lane. The sound was shattering, pieces everywhere, lane blocked to all traffic, and a pissed-off toll attendant. Sisto and I looked at each other, in shock, but an instant later laughter, real belly-laughs. We climbed out of the truck and started throwing the barbeque piece by piece into the back of the truck. We were still laughing uncontrollably as we pulled away. We knew my father was going to have a shit fit when he saw this mess.

We pulled up to his trailer almost two hours after this ordeal began and there he was, on the front porch with a pair of tongs waving at us with a big satisfied smile on his face.

All that quickly changed when he took a look in the bed of the truck. "You idiots! What the hell did you two morons do? I knew I couldn't trust you with this job. I could have trusted a couple of monkeys but not you two clowns!" He told us to go to hell and went back inside to his marinating chicken.

I must've told him, between laughs, that I owed him a new barbeque, because here he was, on my cell phone, holding me to it. "Dad, I'll be down there soon to visit and we can go shopping for one. I didn't forget."

"Okay, Son, I love you, and have a happy birthday. Tell your wife and kids the old man was asking about them."

"Dad, before you go, how's Cookie?" Cookie is his third wife, real nice lady, probably keeping him alive. Maybe it's true that only the good die young. My father should have been dead twenty years ago from all the drugs and alcohol, but somehow he just keeps plugging along.

"She's doing good, considering all that I put her through. I still don't know how she puts up with me every day."

"That's for sure," I tell him. He told me he married Cookie—at the age of seventy-one—just so he could tell her he wants a divorce. My dad has a strange sense of humor to go along with all of his other endearing qualities.

Just for the record, after my mother, who he had five kids with him, my father married Marie (the Step Monster) and they had one child, my little sister, Donna. Every single kid left the house by the age of sixteen. Donna must have been around ten when my father left.

My dad asked me to take a ride with him one day to Pennsylvania. It meant I could see my sister, since that was where she and Marty were living, so I said yes. I thought it would be just the two of us, driving, talking, almost normal. As a kid, I never had a conversation with him so I put a lot of weight into this little road trip. I showed up at his apartment, only to be greeted by this skanky looking woman, about fifteen years younger than him. She had a raspy voice from chain-smoking, skinny legs, tremendous boobs, and a beer belly. All I could think of was, my dad finds her better than us, his own family. She dropped the "F" bomb every other word.

My dad introduced her. "Son, this is Sunny."

I actually had the nerve to ask him what the hell he was doing with this lady and he actually had the nerve to reply, "Son, you have no idea what she can do." I honestly didn't want to know.

Come to find out my father had left Marie and Donna (in the middle of the night, his style) for what he thought were greener pastures. He took all he owned in a paper bag (a family trait: most of us travel light when we're on the run!), and he moved in with this woman that he met in a bar, Sunny.

On the whole drive to PA, Sunny ate Slim Jims. I was getting sick watching her peel Slim Jim after Slim Jim, tossing the wrappers on the floor of the car. It was like she was peeling bananas. We kept having to stop because, as she put it, "These things are going right through me." Whew. Too much information. Then, we'd be back in the car for ten minutes and she would say, "John, you gotta pull over, I need another wiping." Just remembering this now makes me want to puke.

This unfortunate relationship didn't last long. As I predicted, after it ended, my father decided to move in with my older sister Adele, who was living in Pennsylvania at the time. It amazed me that she even took him in, but, as they say, blood is thicker than water, and quite honestly, he was really running out of options.

My sister, knowing she couldn't support him and his bad habits for any great length of time, ended up running an ad in a paper that read, "retired man looking for a companion blah blah blah" and made him look like a real catch, and he got lucky and met Cookie. He ended up moving in with her, and after a couple of years they moved to Florida. So my sister got lucky, and Cookie, well...she got my father. They moved to Florida and that's where they are now.

"Okay, Pops. I love you. We'll talk soon," I say.

"Please call me sometimes and check to see if I'm still alive."

"Okay, Dad, I will," thinking as I said it that guys like him will always survive somehow.

6:53 p.m.

"Philosophy is really nostalgia,
the desire to be at home."
—Novalis

Michelle usually calls me to check in and see if I'll make it home by 7:00 to eat with the family. It's always a priority for me and if I'm running just a bit late, I'll ask her to wait. Sometimes though, I have to miss it. A lot of my sales calls are around the dinner hour, with a husband just getting in from work and his wife wanting to have him there for the consultation. I can run through the important stuff with both homeowners present and then one or the other takes over as my primary contact when the job is underway. Unfortunately, most of those initial meetings take place early evening or weekends. It's the nature of the business. The only other thing that interrupts the family dinner is events that have to do with the kids. We've eaten plenty of meals on the run, on the sidelines and sitting on the tailgate, all due to sports. I guess that even these rushed, brown-bagged meals can count as family meals since, well, and we are all sitting around together enjoying them. I miss those days of baseball and rushed meals. I thought my little guys would never grow into men. I thought I had all the time in the world.

"All the time in the world"… who are we kidding? You live and then you die. Mortality is a tough lesson, but one that naturally comes to mind on a guy's fiftieth. What you did wrong, what you did right, the wisdom to know what you can change, as they say in AA. We do our best if we want our life to count. And I count my blessings; a loving family, good friends, a successful business.

Tonight we put aside our routine. Tonight's special. Michelle made that clear this morning: be home by 7:00 pm.

• • •

I never get tired of pulling up to my house. I always feel lucky to have it. Although it's a small ranch style, we did a little each year for ten years to make it the way it is now. We put in a pool, built a three-car garage, landscaped, finished the basement. Our house is a true reflection of who we are and what we are proud of. My favorite part is the circular drive. It's an impressive entrance. And right in the center is a three-tiered fountain made of concrete, topped off with a pineapple design. The pineapple is the universal symbol of hospitality, and that is the exact message I want to convey, "Welcome, welcome to my humble abode. Come in for a glass of wine or an espresso. Stay! My wife will cook for you!"

It's a miracle that we have the house at all. About seventeen years ago I was renting an apartment upstairs from my in-laws. They decided to sell. Our second child had just been born. Michelle and I had to think fast. At the time I had about $700.00 saved and not a person to borrow money from. I had a job as a salesman working for a friend of my brother.

One day, a guy who happened to own a lot of real estate in our town came into the office. He was a friend of my boss and someone I respected. I explained my situation and asked him if he had anything for rent or a "fixer upper." He gave me an address and when I pulled up to the house, I fell in love immediately. It was run down and in desperate need of repair. My wife said, "No way!" I could understand how, with a toddler and an infant, this house would be an insane undertaking. But I told her, "The sun shines on this house from sun up 'til sundown. Michelle, the only other person to ever live here was a priest. To me, this is a spiritual site. We can make it our home, ours forever."

I called the owner to ask him how much he wanted. The price was out of my range (honestly, anything would

have been out of my range) but he told me that, because he
was tied up in getting permits for his subdivision, he could-
n't sell it to me, anyway. At least, not legally. But if I was
willing to work on the place, and accrue money while I did,
when he was able to sell, he'd sell to me.

I intended to come up with enough money in two
years, about the time it was going to take him to firm up
his subdivisions. Most sane people would call me insane,
putting my heart, soul, and bare hands into a place that I
didn't even own, but I had faith—crazy, irrational faith—
that this was all going to work out.

It was a risk, I know, but we shook on the deal, and I
began renovating the house. Three months after that handshake we moved in. I worked every night. I enlisted every
friend to help. Two years later we had the beginnings of a
masterpiece. The owner called me about the sale, I secured
my loan, and we closed. And what did my wife say? "Make
me one promise, that we never sell this house!" And I re-
sponded, "Don't worry about that!"

Truth be told, one day we probably will sell. The kids
will be gone, we'll downsize and move to the warm
weather, but this will always be my home of happiness. A
handshake was a handshake, and faith got me through that
one, and many more.

• • •

I am actually five minutes early as I pull into the driveway. I see that my sons' cars are in the driveway along with Bran's girlfriend's and, of course, Michelle's car. I'm a little nervous as I climb out of my truck. The front door swings open. "Right on time!" my wife greets me, looking excited. First thing I notice is that her hair is not "done" but instead in her housework ponytail. Maybe I was wrong: maybe there isn't any party. Wait, am I disappointed?

"I got a surprise for you!" Michelle shouts out. For once, her little dog isn't barking at her heels.

"Great!" I muster, and I head in the front door. The dog's on the couch, muzzled. My wife is really pulling out all the stops if she's got that mutt muzzled for my sake. Though this sight, instead of pleasing me, disorients me, like I am in someone else's house, someone else's living room. This must be someone else's dog, he looks so distressed.

I know it's my house because of the painting. That portrait that I pass coming and going, hung over the mantel for maximum visibility. My beautiful mother in her prime, rendered by a sensitive and renowned artist. I like to think she looks down on me, and I accept the light in those painted eyes as a sort of blessing as I move into the house. My wife is behind me, so close I feel claustrophobic. She is pushing me into the kitchen, and I hurry towards it, since I need to put some space between us.

As I enter, I am greeted with a big birthday yell from my sons Chris and Brandon and Bran's girlfriend Katherine. They are already seated at the table, decked with flowers and candles and loads of food. I desperately need air but I manage a "thank you" and reach for a much needed seat. I experience something—a letdown or a relief, I can't tell which—as my wife begins to ramble on and recite every detail of planning and cooking to execute this feast. I feel more like a man facing his last meal. I think I may vomit. I sip my water and breathe deep. I feign a deep interest in her story about hiding food and cooking all day and her mouth is moving but I don't really hear her. I snap back to reality as she tells me, for the second time, "Open the card on my plate!"

"Michelle, everything looks so beautiful and delicious," I say, and my voice sounds like it comes from someone else. I open my card. It shows a guy and a girl from the twenties kissing and it reads, "To A Special Guy on his Special Day." Inside is a handwritten message from my wife: "Fifty gone, fifty more to go. Forever yours, I love you, Michelle."

"Thanks, Babe, it's beautiful."

"Open our card, Dad!" Bran yells, and his girlfriend Katherine and brother Chris concur. I open it and it's a gift certificate for a manicure, pedicure and massage. "Thanks, guys. Really thoughtful. I will enjoy this."

"Plus we've got dinner reservations for tomorrow night!"

"Yeah," adds Michelle. "A night out other than at Carmine's or the social club." She's got to get her jab in. Michelle thinks I'm too settled in my ways.

I let it pass. "Thanks, guys, I'd love that."

I start to get my composure back as Michelle starts filling my plate. I gently ask her to slow down.

"Why? You don't like this?" she asks.

"No," I say. "I just want to pace myself, there's so much here." She's loading up my plate and as the smells are melding together... my lightheadedness returns. What the fuck, I wonder. I thought I didn't want a party. Maybe I did? Damn. I should not have eaten that lunch; she told me she was preparing a feast. The dog rubs his muzzle against my legs. I hang in there, taking little bites, following each with a sip of water. I remind myself of that Asian kid that always wins the Nathan's hot dog eating contest, the one who sticks the hot dogs in the water to help them go down easily. At this thought, my food starts rising in my throat.

"I have to lay down."

"What's wrong with you?" Michelle asks.

"Nothing's wrong."

"This is all your favorites: medium rare prime rib, goat cheese whipped potatoes, and creamed spinach, sautéed mushrooms, caramelized onions."

Just hearing the list makes me woozy. "I'm sorry, Hon." I stand up unsteadily. "Sorry, kids," I say.

"That's okay, Dad."

Chris adds, "More for us!" and everybody laughs.

"We got desserts, too," Michelle adds. "More than one."

That does it. I mutter another apology and stumble out of the room.

Heading down the hallway seems longer than usual. The walls close in. What's wrong with me? All day long I expected this and took it in stride. I'm okay with it being a special day. I'm okay with turning fifty—at least, I tell myself I am. Is it the party? How can it be? The people I love have worked hard to show they love me. What then? Why?

The room spins and it's getting hard to breathe. I can't yell for help. The dog is with me but not barking, as my legs turn to rubber and I reach out but grasp nothing.

I fall and hit the floor.

"Chris."

A voice comes to me, muffled. I'm underwater, submerged in a murky depth. I see shapes but they're unclear, just patches of light and dark.

"Chris."

Then I'm floating up, up, up, a swimmer heading toward an uncertain surface.

"Chris."

I break through.

I am on a couch. Thank God I fell on a couch. I'm not feeling too stable. Wait a minute. I know this couch. This is not the brown leather couch in my living room on Meadowcrest Drive. This is my mother's pullout couch back in the cottage that she lived in when I was a teenager. The same couch where she let me crash when I had nowhere to go. The same couch that I left so abruptly to sow my wild oats in Florida. I am still in my clothes and someone is sitting next to me. I know her.

She's not Michelle.

"Welcome back, Chris," she says.

It's my mother. And she smiles in that beautiful way I love, that smile that radiates enough warmth to heat a house. It's almost too warm... I'm dizzy again.

My mother sits at my feet with one arm set across the back of the couch. Her right leg is tucked underneath her with her left leg dangling. I can see her chipped toenail polish, like a cherry pop red, matching her fingernails, which are bitten to the quick.

I glance around the room and it's just as I remember it. It's a simple, beige haven from rug to walls with a TV in a low wall unit, coffee table, and a couple of chairs, mismatched, and off to the side. An unfinished jigsaw puzzle sits on a table between them. My mother always liked these puzzles, called them her therapy.

Outside the window I see a small deck and beyond it a narrow country road. I always did like it here. Of all the places of my past, this is the place that felt most like home, the place that held the most love for me. But maybe it wasn't the place, maybe it was just that my mother was in it. That's sure what it feels like at this very moment.

I bring my eyes back around to her and she reaches for my hand. I am afraid that if I speak she will disappear but I'm so longing to hear her voice that it pains me.

How long have I been here? How long has she been watching over me? The thought comes to me that it's been my whole life. I want to be here more right now. All that is going through my head is a prayer that I learned as a kid. My grandmother called it The Guardian Angel Prayer. "Angel of God my guardian dear/ To whom God's love permits me here/ Ever this day be at my side/ To light, to guard, to rule, to guide. Amen."

I look up at her beautiful face. "Mom, I know you're dead," I manage to get out. I'm relieved: I can speak and I can hear my voice. And she didn't disappear. "Please don't tell me I died. Please, Mom, I can't leave my family... they need me. You died too young, I always feared this would happen to me, too." I babble, half sobbing, hyper-ventilating.

"Son," she says. "We have some unfinished business to settle. I know it's been haunting you for most of your life."

Oh, God, her voice is melting me. It's hard to breathe and listen at the same time, and every sense seems mo-mentous. I can smell her and the room, I can feel her hand in mine, I can see her face: these things should not be hap-pening.

"Mom, I thought I was getting a party." My thoughts are so scattered right now. "I was happy with..."

"Son," she cuts me off. "It's not that. Look, you're get-ting a rare opportunity here to review your life. So let's go back to the beginning..."

"Mom." Am I whining? I'm a fifty year-old man. "I'm

happy with my life just the way it is."

"Yes, you are, and I'm glad you are. But you always thought you got a raw deal. This thought still imposes itself on your life from time to time. You can't hide from it and you can't hide it from me. Where I am now, I can see you, your past, your present and your future. And I can hear you, not only what you are saying to others, but what you are saying to yourself, your private thoughts."

My head spins. I'm calm and desperate at the same time. I want to be here, where I bathe in my mother's love, and yet I want to be with my family. "Mom, please tell me. Am I dead? You have to tell me or I can't go any further with this."

"No, Son, you're not dead. That's not the plan for you right now. You're just taking a break. Everyone around you is worried right now. But you're fine."

"Oh, thank God. Thank you."

"Now," she says, "relax and let's talk. I don't want to keep you here longer than need be. That pretty wife of yours shouldn't have to worry one minute more than she has to. You're a lucky man, Chris. You've found a woman who loves you dearly. I never loved your father like that, and he never loved me." Hard words to hear, but I know it's the truth.

"I want to answer some of those questions that have been challenging your serenity all these years," she con-

tinues. "First off, how could I have left my children when they needed me so much?" My heart sinks to think that we were starting here, in the most painful stop along my journey of life thus far. The thought of having a mother, a beautiful, loving mother one day, and not having her the next grates at my insides. This is too painful and as much as I want an answer, I don't want to hear it. "At the time I was just human and things weren't as they appeared. This truth is painful but it will set you free. Your dad and I never loved each other like a married couple should, like how you do with Michelle. We never respected each other or valued each other's company. Your dad didn't even want to marry me when I was pregnant with your brother John and I was only sixteen. I told my father, the same man who wouldn't think twice about lashing a strap across my face, and he threw me out. My mother had died at a young age of forty-two, which left me in the care of this horrible, bitter man I could barely consider a father, so I gladly left and moved in with your father's parents."

I know this much so far. She goes on: "Your grandmother Tessy was wonderful to me. She had enough warmth in her to fill the void of mother, father and even the love that a husband should give me. She insisted your father and I get married... it was the fifties and this was the solution, even though we didn't love each other.

"Your father was never around but Tessy was always

there for me. Your father was a drinker, a cheater and an all-around bastard, but your grandmother would straighten him out every so often. He would toe the line for a while but quickly go back to his old ways. This was no way for a young bride and mother to live, but I had Tessy. Your father managed to keep me pregnant and in the care of his parents for a long time. Even your aunts and uncles, his own siblings, lent a hand as he partied more and he and I had more kids."

"Mom, you don't have to tell me this." I see the memory of it all as she tells it, a movie projected on the wall of my mind. It's very painful.

"No, I want to continue. We can't waste a minute of this opportunity." Her hand shakes and her voice trembles as she tells it. "It seemed as if I was pregnant for five straight years. I had no break. Your Aunt Barbara and Uncle Joe helped me along with the constant assistance from Tessy."

"Mom, please stop." I see the pain on her face.

"No," she says sternly. "I've waited decades to tell you all of this. This is my unfinished business as well as yours."

I try to stay focused and absorb what she's saying. The circumstances are strange enough, just having her in front of me. But hearing her speak, seeing her pain... it's suffocating. But I can't risk it ending.

My mother continues. "By the time I was twenty-

three, I had five kids and barely a husband. There was no time to sit and bemoan my situation. I worked from sun up to sun down, keeping you all clean and fed, and let that take up my time. Trying to keep you happy, too, and unaware. Kids shouldn't have to grow up in that turmoil.

"The years went by until on one particular Christmas, it all became too clear and too much to handle. I had just learned that your father was having an affair with a friend of ours from the neighborhood. Everyone knew about it, except me, of course. I felt like a fool. He had always been a cheater but this was right in front of my face, for everyone to see. I was never so embarrassed. He had crossed the line and I couldn't handle it. I had a nervous breakdown from the stress of the affair, the shame, the pressure of taking care of all these children. I confronted him and asked for a divorce. It was a week before Christmas and I wanted to get through the holiday for the sake of you kids. I wanted him to move out after Christmas." She pauses to catch her breath.

"My plan was simple, or so I thought. I figured it would make him happy. He'd be free to carry on with his affairs and I, with the help of some friends, would be able to raise my kids without having to put up with his bullshit.

"Well, asking for the divorce didn't sit well with him. His drinking escalated and by Christmas morning the shit hit the fan. He had already told me that he would kill me *before he let me take his kids from him. I just assumed it was the liquor talking. But by 10:00 a.m. he was acting crazy. He came to me and said, ironically, 'You're not breaking up this family.' I said, 'Let's not do this today.' But he got more and more enraged. I told him that I was going to call his brother to come over here and control him. And with that, he grabbed a knife from the kitchen drawer and tried to cut my throat. I put up my hand in defense and he almost cut my thumb off. That's when you and Dominic came into the kitchen. You heard the commotion and came running in and you both started yelling and crying and tugging on your dad to get him to stop attacking me. I broke away, ran out of the house knowing he had a gun at his disposal. Sure enough, he came after me, gun in hand just as the cops showed up, and they took him away."*

"But, Mom. Why didn't they keep him in jail? I mean, he tried to kill you. I remember it all clearly now. He was going to kill you!"

"I didn't press charges. For Tessy's sake, I didn't press charges. Your grandmother promised me she would straighten him out. She convinced me it was best for you kids, too, not to have a father in jail for attempted murder. They did their best to talk me into seeing things their way. They convinced me that I was doing what was best for you kids.

"My brother Brandon took all you kids to Uncle Tom's for a couple of days. I'm not sure if you remember that. Your father knew every cop and judge in town and they let him off with a slap on the wrist and turned a blind eye. You kids came back, your father promised we would work it all out like adults and life would go on.

"Well, life did go on and in a blink, your father was drunk again. It was the middle of the night, you kids were asleep, and he told me that the next time he would 'finish the job.' This was no empty threat. He told me to take my clothes and get out. I had no choice. I had been through this before. There was no happy ending with me in the picture. It was the hardest thing I ever did, the hardest thing a mother could do, and it tortured me the rest of my life. If I stayed, he would have killed me. You'd have no mother and certainly no father either. I could barely take care of myself, let alone five kids. The only choice was to leave and hope that between your father's family and his mother you would all be well taken care of.

"But no one cares for kids like their own mother. Your father ruined me for that. The real miracle is that you all survived your horrific upbringing, some better than others, but you all survived. So many things went wrong for you, you didn't deserve any of it, and you didn't stand a chance. And yet, here you are, full of life, full of friends and family, a successful businessman, a great father and

---

husband, a wonderful son."

Hearing her tell it, I relive the whole story. I watch it unfold before my eyes in all its horrific detail.

"*Sometimes you need a turn or two in the river for the journey to be worth something,*" *my mother says.* "*So many things had to go wrong for your life to be so right. What I am here to tell you is that, although it was painful, it turned out to be the best thing for you.*"

So much pain, so much to absorb. In the pause, I sit up straight on the couch. I clear my throat. My shirt is wet. I realize I'm crying. "*Mom, if you and Dad worked it out and stayed together, I probably would have gone to college, done something great with my life.*" *I try to digest all that she says, memories flying back to me. Her words unleash so much within me.* "*I feel like I wasted so much time trying to find myself and rid myself of the pain from my childhood.*"

"*The pain is what made you the person you are today. That pain gave you your compassion for others, and it provided you with your clear understanding of the world around you, of your deep understanding for all things. It motivated you to find God and become a spiritual person. You read all of those books. Remember 'You gotta lose your mind to find it'? That was your process. What you've always thought is that your life would have been better if we all—your father, me, you kids—stayed together. That's not true, you see... that's just a fantasy, an unrealistic picture society paints for us. It's unfair. Sure, life can be terrific for those families with two loving parents who live in a house with a white picket fence and a dog, but even they have problems. They're maybe just better equipped to work through their challenges, battles their obsessions and addictions, control their tempers and their urges. Your father and I, we were not so well-equipped. And for that reason, we were better apart. God knows what you witnessed during your young life. God only knows what more unholy things you would have witnessed if we stayed together even one more day."*

Deep down I know she's right but I refuse to believe it. I don't want to see the bad, I only want to pretend it could all be good. Aren't parents supposed to make everything all better, kiss the wound and make it go away? For me, the wound didn't disappear, my mother did. My childhood did.

"Chris, listen to me." My mother said. "Your life was predestined. The basic framework was put in place at your birth. It was up to you how it would play out and you handled what life threw at you beautifully. You are exactly where you should be... in my eyes, in your eyes, in God's eyes.

"A river turns to the right and to the left. No direction is the wrong one. Some turns lead to deep, easy flowing

waters and some to shallow, murky ones. It's just how it flows to get to its destiny, smooth and rough, alternating along its path. Your role is to jump in and let it take you. You always have. Truly let go and trust God, flow with the river, and enjoy it. Enjoy the smooth parts, the rocky parts and even the rapids, knowing that if you continue to go with it and resist fighting it, it will be a fulfilling ride to your destiny, in the end, cradled in the arms of the Lord."

As I stare at her, still not believing that she's in front of me, this apparition I've longed for so long, I realize my mother's disappearance was a turn in the river. My siblings moving away was another. But these rough turns led to smooth turns, of meeting my friends, my wife, the births of my boys.

"Look at what happened each time your father forced you to move. With each new town came, yes, another dismal house. But also your best friends, your lifelong relationships that you value so much. Meeting your wife is a result of such a move, settling in this town, marrying, raising kids, building a business, all byproducts of turns in the river. Believe it or not, it's all part of a perfect plan, a plan that seemed so imperfect in the making yet yielded so much good and happiness. It taught you love and hope and to seek happiness. Sometimes it seems that things are all going wrong, but in truth, they need to go so wrong in

order to turn out right in the end.

"Chris, never give up hope and always believe that there is a master plan at work. You must trust in this."

"Mom, really, did you actually push me where I am? Did you set this plan in motion?" I want to say so much but I'm struggling to organize my thoughts. "Mom, I really wish you were around to meet my kids. They're so great. You would love them."

"I do love them, I do know them intimately. I've watched them grow up. I am so proud of the father you've become, even that is a result of your past. You are always trying to give your kids the love and the life that you feel you missed out on. You ask, did I push you in the right direction? Well, it kind of works like this... we can line you up with the river, but it's up to you to jump in and let go. We can even push you in the river, if at times you need a push, but it is up to you to either latch on to rocks or tree limbs and never let go, fighting the current the whole way, clinging to safety. But by holding on you would not end up where you are supposed to, you would just stay stuck and struggling in one place. We could then send up a storm to push you away from those rocks, to release your grasp on that tree limb, but you would have to release your grip knowing it's going to be a rough ride. Again, if you just let go on your own accord, your own terms, it's the easiest way to end up where you should be."

"Mom, I need a drink of water. Can I get up, move around, or will all of this—" I gesture to my surroundings, even engulfing my mother in the sweep of my arms— "disappear?"

"Just stand up, it will be fine, it will feel like marshmallows. Take a moment to steady yourself."

It's hard to believe that I've been lying down the whole time. Has it even been a long time? My mother laughs at my awkwardness as I try to stand up.

She slaps the couch. "Let's fold up this old thing so that we can sit on it together."

I reach behind the couch for the cushions, expecting them to be there as they were many years ago. I'm not disappointed.

I walk into the kitchen and open the cabinet to grab two water glasses. The faucet sticks a bit, just like it used to, and I fill the glasses. Could water from a certain place have a particular taste? I think so. I am experiencing a rush of memories, through sight, smell, and taste. Even the scratchiness of the couch fabric in the other room is freaking me out, it's so familiar.

My mother follows me into the kitchen. She watches me the whole time. I hand her a glass of water. She looks so calm and at ease with this whole strange situation.

"I needed that," I say after a long draw on my glass. I feel so much better. I'm actually relaxing a bit. There is, however, a tugging in my brain, a calling of sorts, but I am choosing to ignore it for the time being.

Without warning, my mother leans in with a kiss on my cheek and a hug. God, that feeling, so long ago lost, comes rushing back. Can a person who is presumably passed out (because I know that on some plane I am unconscious) possibly feel like he is going to pass out? I'm just trying to hold back my tears.

We walk together back into the living room, which used to be my bedroom. I look around, my eyes darting back and forth, fixing on particular items. I remember this house so well. There are photos of me and my brothers and sisters on the bookcases and side tables. I look at them all and we head back to the couch. I take my place but she chooses to sit across from me.

"Come sit here, Mom. I want you next to me."

"I want to look at you, Chris. Although this feels really great," she says, "we have limited time. That is, if you want to go back to your current life." She laughs. "We need to stay on track. There are some things you need to absorb before you go back. Your beautiful family, your wife, your kids— they're all probably worried sick by now."

"Do I have to go back?" I wonder.

"You want to, don't you?"

I hate to admit it, but I wish I could stay here, with

her, forever.

"*I want to take you on a journey of how your life, so harsh and challenging, ended up so great in the end,*" *my mother says. "Every time you moved, you thought it was a bad thing. It made you angry and sad. But let's look back at it. Each move was another twist or turn in the river of your life. You wouldn't have all your best friends today if you didn't keep moving. You wouldn't have met Tim and then Joe K and then Big Joe and his brother, Cosmo. And your partner Kevin and so many other people that loved you and mentored you along the way. All of these people, they are all part of the plan and it's much bigger than that. Because not even you can see how many others you have touched and influenced along the way. Your understanding of pain, your firsthand experience, made their lives better. All the years you were reading spiritual books and making an effort to see God, your life was going great. You felt great, your businesses prospered, all was good.*

"*But then came a time when you stopped reading, when you began to take all the credit for the good things, the money, and you became self-absorbed. What happened then? I watched you. You got really sick. Your self-absorption brought on a physical illness. You developed seizures, anxiety, and stomach problems. Your tension and sleepless nights drove you right back to the hand of*

God and you returned to a happy and healthy life. You learned the hard way that life is always better when you stand in the light of the Lord. When you step out of the light, you stand in darkness. Life becomes bleak.

"I love you, Son, and I'm glad that we got this opportunity to spend this time together but please remember, don't be afraid to share the love you feel. I know that, in the past, you've held back showing all the love you feel for fear of being hurt. I know that you felt that if your own mother could leave you, then who can't? But please, fear nothing and love everybody. And to answer one of your big questions, even if your father and I loved each other and you grew up in the perfect home, you wouldn't have gone to college. Just like your son Brandon, who grew up in a perfect home with a perfect childhood. So please, don't be mad at him for not pursuing further education. He's going to be successful just like you. Both of your boys are destined for greatness. Listen, college isn't for everybody, but love and God, which are the same things, are. So, teach your boys that lesson, and you will be giving them the greatest gift of all. And lead by example. A man of great faith and great love is better than any certificate.

"One thing about the river, Chris: it twists and it turns but it is always pure. It has an inlet and an outlet, which assures a steady flow. It does not become unmoving or stagnant, like a pond may, but instead, its move-

ments, both harsh and smooth, keep it pure and ever-changing. Don't become stagnant by holding onto things, clinging to thoughts and feelings that can way you down. Keep your thoughts flowing, let them be organic in their movement in and out of your mind, let go and trust in God. Don't become a human pond where things fester and cause disease. Everything is going to be okay. Step back and see God's work in everything. There are no coincidences. Like the woman who did my portrait, and know that I will be alongside of you every step of the way."

Her portrait. Yes, my constant reminder of her beauty.

As she is saying this, she is sliding closer to me on the couch where I can almost touch her. I reach my hand out to have a moment of physical contact as her image is starting to fade.

I start yelling, "Mom! Mom! I love you, I love you!" But I can no longer see her clearly. As her image fades away, and so does the sound of her voice, trailing…"Chris, I love you too."

7:32 p.m.

"Chris?"

"Dad?"

I open my eyes. My wife and two sons hover over me, their faces barely containing their terror. I'm lying in my bed.

"Honey, are you okay?" my wife keeps repeating. "Are you okay?" She says something about calling an ambulance.

I begin to cry. "I'm okay," I tell her. "I don't need an ambulance. "But tell me...what happened?"

"We were in the kitchen and heard a bang. I came up the hall and found you lying on the floor. I yelled for the boys and they helped me lift you and we put you on the bed. You were mumbling incoherently. Then you shouted 'I love you, I love you!' and you came to."

I see the fright and confusion in my wife's eyes.

"Were you yelling to me?" she asks.

"Yes." I lie. That's the easiest way right now. I am too

disoriented to get into an explanation of what I just experienced. How could I possibly begin to explain something that I myself don't understand? "No ambulance, I feel better. How long was I out?"

"Not long," Michelle reassures me.

"Dad, what can we do for you?" Chris looms over me, his face anxious. Brandon and his girlfriend Katherine are right behind him.

"I'm okay. I just want to rest," I say. "Just for a bit."

Michelle places her hand on my forehead. "Then I'm coming back in to check on you again. I'll bring you some water."

"I'm fine, believe me. It's just the excitement of my birthday. I definitely ate 'way too much today." I just want to be left alone.

With them gone, I think about my dream. Was it a dream? It was so real. I'm completely wiped out, like I've been dragged around and beaten up. I'm sore all over. Could it really have only been a couple of minutes? It felt like an hour. Now the question is popping into my head. Why am I drawn to the clock at 11:11? Or 1:11? I know she died on January eleventh, so I always think of her when those numbers are on the clock, like I'm nudged to look. I keep running through our conversation about the river. What she said, it all makes sense. Was it really her? It had to be her. I wish I had more time. I woke up too soon.

My wife enters again with my water. I apologize for lying in bed like this after all of the work she did to make my birthday. She tells me not to worry, to rest, and she will come back after she cleans up the kitchen.

"Thanks, Hon," I say to her.

"Chris?"

I look up at her.

"I love you too." I'm startled. Then I remember my lie, my "I love you!" when I came to.

Michelle gives me a tender kiss on my lips, so sweet, so soft, so full of love that my heart swells. The tears well up again, and to spare my embarrassment, my wife leaves the room and gently closes the door behind her.

8:13 p.m.

"You slept a little," Michelle says. She holds a glass of water under my lips to sip. "The boys don't want to go out before singing to you. They want you to blow out your candles, maybe have some cake."

How is cake supposed to make me feel better? I need my comfortable sweats, I need to be left alone. But I rouse myself, better make her happy, and better let the boys see that I am all right. I know that I gave them a scare.

Michelle follows close behind as I head down the hallway and recall that marshmallow feeling I had earlier. Better not tell anyone about that. It's too weird to explain.

Everyone is gathered in the kitchen, concern on their faces. On the island is a huge, beautiful cake, candles lit. "It's such a pain in the ass to make a gluten-free carrot cake, but nothing's too good for my honey," Michelle says. She's always so worried that her baking won't come out perfect, but it does every time. She has also made chocolate dipped strawberries, another of my favorites.

Michelle takes three or four attempts at getting the photo just right (my son Chris is about to lose his mind in frustration), and I blow out the candles after everyone sings. My mind is so muddled that I forget to make a wish.

"This is all amazing," I say with as much enthusiasm that I can muster. But really, the last thing I want to do is eat. I can tell the kids are itching to get on with their Friday night plans. They've been sitting around while I've been sleeping, so I say, "Okay, guys, let's cut this cake, and then everybody give me a hug and a kiss and get outta here!" And I mean every word of this as I work my way around to all of them. As they leave, I taste my sliver of cake and my strawberry and give my wife a big hug. I tell her, "This cake is so good, it's ridiculous!" She beams with satisfaction and I head back to my bed to lie down while she, once again, is left to clean up the kitchen.

11:11 p.m.

I must have nodded off again, I feel as if I am being nudged awake, my wife is nowhere in sight as I glance over to my bedside clock. I can hear the TV from the living room and I think, "What is going to happen next? This can't be a coincidence." I return to sleep, a dreamless sleep, for which I am actually relieved.

The next day

9:33 a.m.

I wake up late. Michelle must have turned off my alarm, a very nice gesture, but one that stresses me out knowing that I am already late beginning my day.

Putting yesterday's events behind me, I get up, pour coffee and peek in on boys. They're still sleeping. It must have been a late night; I never heard them come in.

I go through my morning routine feeling somewhat disconnected. I take out the garbage. Michelle must be at the gym. I look at the dog; even he's sensitive to me today and keeping quiet. I am anxious to get out of the house. I leave and make none of my usual stops on my way to the office.

9:52 a.m.

I immediately head straight upstairs and check messages. I have to get this day back onto a normal footing. Everything feels off kilter. I think about my mother and look towards her picture. It's face down. What the hell? What forces are at work here? What are they trying to tell me? I break out in a sweat. Should I welcome all of this? Should I fear it? Should I just ignore it and move forward? She must be trying to reach me, to let me know that last night was real. To assure me that it happened but that it's all okay.

I am jolted out of my thoughts by the phone ringing.

It's Michelle. "Hi, Honey. How are you feeling?" There's not too much concern in her voice, which leads me to think that I am putting way too much emphasis on this whole thing.

"I'm feeling pretty good today. Not sure what happened last night. Sorry if I spoiled things."

"Not at all. I'm more concerned about you. Should I

make a doctor's appointment for you? The boys are worried. It could be as simple as exhaustion, or maybe anxiety or even high blood pressure. Either way, you should go. Better to be safe than sorry. Look how many in our age group are dropping like flies."

"Our age group"? Was she trying to make me feel better with her little joke?

"And remember," she continues. "Dinner tonight at Mama Rosa's, where we had your dad's party a few years ago."

"Okay, Mama Rosa's, 6:00 pm. I'll meet you there. I'm getting a late start and time is tight today."

"No, come home before, shower, freshen up. I want us to go there together. The boys will meet us there. They want to take their own cars so they can head out straight from there."

What I really need is to visit Big Joe, light up a cigar, and completely unwind for a little while. I just want to go back to normal, help Joe cook for a regular Saturday night, go meet the family for dinner, and then go back and hang with the guys. Just a regular Saturday night. I need routine right now, I need normal! Well, maybe Michelle could just drop me there after. I could always catch a ride home with Coz later on. We'll see how this plays out.

• • •

I ring Big Joe from the car as I am making my daily rounds. "Cool Cat, where you at?" I sing out as he answers the phone.

"I got my son with me," he says, a fair warning to watch myself because I'm on speaker. "We're heading to the Mall. Gotta get him something nice to wear tonight."

"Hi, Uncle Chris!" Little Joe calls out.

"Tonight? What's tonight?" It's strange that Joe would be deviating from the regular "Saturday night with the guys" thing.

"My mom's birthday," (that's right, I think: Mrs. R and I are a day apart), "I promised her a big dinner out with the family. By the way, how was your birthday evening? I know Michelle must have gone all out."

"Crazy story for another time. Listen, good luck shopping at the morgue—ha, I mean mall." (More stores are closing in our local mall faster than are opening; times are changing.) "If you're near Mama Rosa's, stop in. I'll be there with my family. I was actually gonna try to meet up with you guys at the bar later, but it sounds like we'll both be out. Better warn the rest of the guys that you and I are not around! *Ciao!*"

"Not so fast," Big Joe says. "I'll call Nick at Mama Rosa's, move my family dinner over there, and then you and I can leave together. Makes everyone happy, especially us! *Ciao,* my brother. See you later. And bring your Communion money, cuz we got a night of cards ahead of us!"

I laugh as he disconnects. OK, now things are heading back to normal.

As I drive I can't help but think about my whole journey. There have been ups and downs, and turns in the river all along. Maybe my mom was right. Maybe I *am* on course. I do have a good life, a stable life, a great family, and great friends. Really, what more is there? And the truth is, I always hated school. Who am I kidding about the whole college thing? I wouldn't have lasted a day. I was too anxious, just itching to get out there and make my million. I could have never put that off for four more years.

All the guilt I went through, all the blame I placed on others, left little room for true emotion, I was scrambling so much. I was too busy trying to work out life to work out what emotion to feel.

To be precise, the emotion is love. Maybe it wasn't all my stepmother's fault. I just wasn't prepared for someone to replace my real mother. What kid is ever prepared for that? I was pretty cold to this replacement... even now, looking back, I can barely consider her worthy in the least to replace my real mother. I am sure she felt bad when I refused my father's request that I call her "Mom." But calling her "Step Monster" was probably crossing the line. I mean, she was hardly to blame for all of the dysfunction in our household. She may have added to it, not helped it all, but the dysfunction was there before she arrived on the scene. I probably owe her an apology... in some crazy way, her hideous behavior was in response to my hideous behavior. But then again, I was the kid, and she was the adult. Though, I could have been good, at the very least better than I was. I could have given her a chance. This is a revelation, one of many that I am suddenly experiencing.

Now I begin thinking how I might have hurt people along the way. How with my lashing out and fighting, all against the tide, not realizing that things were going my way, but that I was my own worst enemy. Situations were at play, lining up to construct my great life, and I couldn't see it. I was too young, too dumb and self-centered to realize that my problems, my challenges, as bad as they were, were camouflaging a beautiful future. Why couldn't my mother have come to me sooner? Why couldn't she enlighten me and saved me years of emotional struggles and resentments? Why couldn't she show me all of this years ago, instead of now? She's right. I have always held back my feelings. What the hell have I been afraid of? What more could have happened if I had just shared all my fears and anxieties, instead of running and hiding from them? What does it matter now? What can anybody do to me now? Is it too late to change? Is it only a matter a time before they lower me into the ground in a box? And when I'm in that pine box, will I see my mother? My Aunt Barbara?

My grandmother? I only seem to miss the women in my life. Is it their approval I am striving for? Or is it their love that I miss? Is this another revelation? What am I still hiding from? And why hide, after all?

• • •

I wrap up my paperwork for the day. I actually wonder how productive I really was today, not sure if I've even made a phone call. The passing of time has been playing tricks on me and is tiring me out.

I lock up the office and start to head home. I remember the plan: get home and freshen up, change and head to dinner, separate car from the kids. I am tired already. My Bluetooth rings in...it's Timbo. "What's up, Cool Cat?" I answer.

"Yo, man," he says. "Did you forget about me?"

Oh shit, I think. Another call I forgot to make. Like I didn't have other things on my mind. "I worked all day, y'-know," I say. "You could have called me too." My mood has made me defensive. Here I am lashing out at the guy who made a long trip in just to see me.

"Yeah, okay, just wanted to say again, that was a great lunch yesterday. So good to hang out with you and the guys."

"Better for me because you were there, Tim." My mood softens. "I hope you're gonna be at Joe's tonight. I have something with the family first but then I'm heading out and over to Joe's. I'll be at Mama Rosa's first. Joe has something, too, but may bring his family dinner to Mama Rosa's as well. Come by, we'll all cut out of there together. Just like the old days when we'd ditch the girls on a Saturday night!"

"Could be a plan. I'll see what my mom was planning and I'll do my best. Either way, I'll see you at Joe's. Later, Cool Cat."

"Later, Cool Cat!"

As I turn the bend of my favorite church I silently will my mother to give another sign to let me know that everything that happened—her visit, her advice—really happened. Something concrete. I can be patient.

I pull into the driveway, and see the boys' cars are already gone. Pickles the dog flies out of the house barking like he's been shot out of a cannon. My wife comes out after him but all I notice is that she's dressed like she's going to a ball, in a low cut cocktail dress. She looks gorgeous, but very high class. What's going on here? Have I underestimated the significance of tonight's dinner?

"How are you feeling?" she asks as she pecks my cheek. The dog in her hands is nipping at me as she gets close to me.

"Good," I say. "You look great, but..." I hesitate so as not to offend, "... but we're only going to Mama Rosa's."

"Can't I look nice sometimes? On a special occasion?" She's uptight, so I say no more and head straight to my room.

I go through the motions: Wash up, dress, add sports jacket for good measure. Hair brushed. She's pacing downstairs. I hear the clicking of her heels on the foyer tile. I'm getting anxious and I've no clue why.

"OK, Honey, I'm ready," I yell down. "I'll meet you in the car." I have to get her out of the house, she's making me crazy.

I splash on some cologne, the finishing touch, and head out myself. But in the foyer I freeze. My mother's portrait stops me. She looks as she always has (how could she not? Painting's don't change)... but I detect something else in her expression tonight: a satisfaction, and a caution in her eyes. *Remember what I told you, Chris,* she seems to say. And I answer out loud: "How can I know it was real, Mom? How can I know?"

The horn honking outside jolts me back to reality.

In the car Michelle asks, "What took you so long? I could see you standing in the living room, just staring at the wall. And were you talking to yourself? You really are acting very strange."

"It's that portrait of my mother. Stops me every time." I start the car and put it in gear. "I'm fine. This whole goddamned birthday thing is wearing me down. I'm out of balance."

Michelle pats my hand. "Relax. You're right. It's been a busy few days. Let's just enjoy this night of family."

"Y'know, it was so strange, how I met that woman Mary—it's got to be twenty years ago by now—and how we talked and learned about each other's lives, how she painted that portrait of my mother and insisted on giving it to me. I mean, she was a professional portrait painter! She insisted the gift was more for her, to be able to pass on comfort and peace to someone else suffering a loss, just like she was missing her own father. It's funny how we meet certain people just when we're meant to meet them. It's like they're placed in our path and it's up to us to make the connection."

"Wow." Michelle sat back. "You're getting pretty philosophical on me right now. Are you having some kind of midlife crisis?" she asks half joking, but there's concern in her voice. I can tell that she'd love nothing more then to have an ordinary car ride, maybe chat about the usual BS of everyday life.

But I need to continue on my introspective thread.

"Michelle, would you think I was crazy if I told you I had an encounter with my mother?"

"Chris, what do you mean by 'encounter'?"

"Last night when I collapsed I went into some spirit world. I know this sounds nuts, but let me finish. It's the timeframe that's got me confused. You said I was out for

not even two minutes but I spent at least a half hour visiting with my mom. It's hard to explain, but we talked,
touched, engaged in a visit that had to last more than two
minutes. She told me things, answered questions, gave me
advice and insight as if we were sitting around and having
a casual Sunday visit. This is so crazy, but she told me
things that I couldn't make up... that's what's baffling me."

Thank goodness my body can navigate to Mama
Rosa's on cruise control, because I was so focused I was
barely conscious of driving. "She told me the whole story
of my parents' breakup. She talked about my childhood.
She explained to me how, while everything seemed so
tragic, it was all predestined, part of a master plan to get
me here, with this life, with these people." I gesture my
arms wide spread to indicate not only my immediate family
but my friends as well. Michelle understands my gesture,
but she grabs the wheel for fear of going off the road.

"Chris," she says, "at least don't be driving when you
tell me this. You're very emotional."

I pull over to the shoulder of the road and stop. Traffic
zips by beside us. "What's really crazy," I continue, "is that
I remember the entire conversation, word for word."

And I tell my wife about my mother's comparing life
to a river. As I tell it, the words affect me deeply. I fill up
and yet I can't stop telling her. "My mother told me, 'Don't
fight it, it's gonna be what it's gonna be'. Strange, right?"

I don't know what I expected for a response. But Michelle answers, wiping a tear, "Pretty profound. What else did she say?"

I try not to lose my momentum. I continue. I sound rational—at least to myself— and lay the rest of it out: how what seems to be going so wrong can turn out so right; how turns in the river bring us to ourselves.

"And she told you all of this in the less than two minutes you were lying on the floor." Michelle states it, doesn't ask it.

"Yes! It's crazy, right? And now, I'm struggling to make sense of it all. There's not one shred of evidence to convince me this all was real, except that I know it happened. What I need is a sign... I've been waiting for some sign to validate all of this. I was convinced there would be one, but now I am convinced that this is all just plain crazy. I've told you for years she was guiding me and giving me nudges, getting my attention with the time on the clock or that picture in the office. There's got to be something to it."

"Okay..." Michelle says. She's hesitating, and I see she doesn't know what to say. We're on the shoulder of the road about a hundred yards from our destination. Too close to abandon our plans, clock ticking, people waiting. And why abandon our plans anyway? No one is sick or hurt. Michelle says, "Chris, maybe the sign will come, maybe it won't, but no matter what really happened, something *did* happen. But let's get back to reality. We have a nice dinner planned. Let's lighten up and enjoy it. This means a lot to the kids."

"You're right," I reply. The mood has changed. Maybe she doesn't believe a word of what happened to me. I could hardly blame her. Maybe she doesn't know what to make of it. Best to leave it alone.

We pull into the restaurant parking lot. It's crowded, there's barely a spot. So I head around to the right, in the far back.

"Michelle, do you want to get out in front, I can drop you off?"

"No, I'm fine. Isn't that Joe's truck? What's he doing here?"

"I told him we'd be here. He was taking his mother out for dinner so I told him to come here and join us."

"Can't we just once, just one single time, do something as a family?"

"Relax, Michelle. He is family, and it's my birthday."

We enter the restaurant and are greeted by the Eddie, the *maître d'*. "Hello, Chris, Michelle. Happy birthday, Chris! So nice to see both of you." Eddie is a real pro, making a point to remember Michelle's name, even though I usually come stag for my dinners here. "I'll show you to your table."

We pass the bar and continue on past the main dining

room. We head into a small private room. "Since Joe was here with his family, we put you all in the private dining room, a real family gathering. I hope you approve."

"Eddie," I say, "I couldn't have asked for anything better. Thank you so much. I know Nick prefers to keep us hidden from the general public. We can get loud."

Eddie laughs. "Are you kidding, Chris? You guys are good for business, people see and hear you having fun and they want to be a part of it!"

Michelle and I walk into a room already alive with laughter and loud voices. My boys are already there with their girlfriends and Joe has his arm around one of the girls giving his usual line to Chris... "The only reason this pretty young lady hangs around with you is to get to me!" Then he tells his own son, "Jo Jo, meet your new mother." Jo Jo, who's fourteen year old, chuckles at this, but I happen to know that divorce has been hard on the kid. Cosmo and Marcie are there and Marcie, in her sister-in-law voice, tells Big Joe to "Shut up, you idiot!" Joe's mom looks happy. Everybody looks happy. This room has good energy.

I give everyone one big Hollywood hello, like they used to close with on The Dating Game, a blow of a kiss with a big arm wave. It's my signature large group greeting. I can't go around and hug and kiss each person, after all; well, maybe just Joe's mom. Michelle does the person-to-person greetings. It gives her a chance to see what everyone is wearing, comment on weight loss or gain, and discuss recent changes to hairstyles. They compare handbags and shoes as she makes her rounds. Michelle falls right into it without missing a beat, and I'm glad our recent conversation didn't trip up her mood.

Joe had already ordered appetizers, plenty of hot and cold. Cosmo rubs it in my face that I can't eat the Italian bread, "Boy, this stuff is amazing, a little olive oil, some roasted peppers, heaven on a plate."

Food, and friends, stories, insults, jokes, and love, in its own crazy way, a perfect storm. "So, my wife saw your car in the parking lot, Joe, and she wasn't happy." I had to stick it to her, give her the business. Our friends wouldn't recognize us if I wasn't busting her chops.

"Yeah, I was pissed, but then he told me you brought your mom, so I cut him a break." Michelle addresses Joe's mother. "It's so nice to be here with you, Mrs. R., not that rude son of yours!" More laughs. I got to hand it to my wife; she gives it as good as she gets it. We are a perfect match. "But Tim too, what's this all about?" Tim was in the mix, I was so glad to see him. I was feeling guilty about our less than enthusiastic exchange earlier.

"Give me a break, Michelle, my mother sends her regards!" Tim tries to save his ass from my wife's quick tongue lashing.

"Come here, Tim. You know I love you." Michelle embraces him in a warm hug and musses his hair.

Someone asks Tim how his mom is doing. He answers, "Great. Though she swears that her hair turning gray is from the shit we used to put her through when we were kids. I tell her 'Mom, everyone's hair is turning gray, you're getting old,' and she tells me, 'My hair started turning gray the day you met those boys of yours' (he does a great imitation of her voice). Chris, you know she means you!"

I laugh at this because she's probably right.

I excuse myself and head for the restroom. I walk through the bar just to take in the sights. An older woman walks towards me, exiting the restroom. She's tall and attractive, dressed for a night out. As we pass, she looks me dead in the eyes and stops short. She says, "Hi!"

I return the greeting. Do I know her? There's something so familiar about her.

She says, "I know I know you from somewhere."

"I have one of those familiar faces," I say. "You sure?"

"Yes," she says. "I know it will come to me and when it does, I'll find you!"

"Good, because if I stand out here, Nick's gonna need a mop and bucket. I'm in the private room. Feel free to come right in." And I hastily head into the restroom. Crazy, I think. But I meet a lot of people in my business and most of them are local. I do know her from somewhere. Soft eyes, gentle voice, definitely know her, I'm thinking.

As I head back to dinner, I glance in the bar to get another look at that woman. She's about sixty, maybe seventy, and sitting with a couple of other ladies around her age. It'll come to me.

Back in the room, the food is flowing like the Barbarians are at the gate. Nick takes special care of us but we'll all need to see a cardiologist in the morning.

Michelle rises from her chair and comes to my side. Nick stands at the door, overseeing his masterpiece as I come up next to him.

"Cool Cat, you really outdid yourself tonight. It's like we're going to the electric chair!" We embrace in a bear hug. "Man, this food is amazing, thank you so much."

"For you, my friend, the sky's the limit," Nick tells me.

Eddie enters. "Enjoying everything, Chris?"

"The best, Eddie, the best!"

"Hey, Chris, there's a woman out there, asking your name, wanted to know who you are."

"Oh, yeah?" my wife says, and takes my arm off from around her. "A woman, huh?"

I laugh. "Eddie!" I say. "Save me here?"

"Mrs. Scalera," Eddie says. "I'm sure she's not threat to you. You know how your husband's a local celebrity."

Nick teases, "Yes, it must be hard being Mrs. Vinyl King. That makes you The Vinyl Queen!"

Michelle, still playing along, crosses her arms and

plays cool. But I pull her back in. "Seriously though, Eddie, I saw her. She must be a customer of mine. I know her but I can't seem to place her."

"Actually, I told her your name and her eyes welled up with tears. I think she wanted to cry, but hey, I'm no expert when it comes to women. I just thought you should know."

"How bad could the job have been?" I joke again but this news jolted me. Really? Tears? What the hell?

"Chris, you should go out there and talk to her," my wife tells me.

I head out, and the woman is already waiting by the door. "Hello again," she says, "You don't remember me. I'm Mary. I painted your mother's portrait."

This cold buzz runs through me. "Oh, my God." That's all I can reply. She's older, sure, but so am I. Of course it's her. How could I not recognize her?

"I tried to find you to tell you about something," Mary says. "But I forgot your name, and I couldn't find your business card anywhere."

"The Vinyl King?"

"No, you were something different."

"Right," I manage to choke out. "I was in a different business then. I was called The Blind Man."

"No, that doesn't ring a bell, either," she says.

"Wait. I was helping a guy named Bobby. It wasn't my job at all. I was there helping and you invited us into your house for a cold drink."

"That's it!" Mary exclaims. "I knew it'd come to one of us!"

"Mary," I say. "I look at that that portrait every time I come into or go out of my house. I have it over the mantel so I can't miss it. In fact, I was looking at it before I came here tonight. I mean really looking at it, and I thought about you and how we met. Can you believe this coincidence?"

"I don't believe in coincidences," Mary says. "I have something crazy to tell you. Remember years ago when we met?"

I nod. "Yes. I remember it well. It has been at least twenty years."

"I told you the story of how I lost my father at a young age, in a car accident. It happened on his way home from work and he was pronounced dead at the scene. I told you how I wished I could have had the opportunity to say goodbye and tell him what a great father he'd been. I told you my whole story. You were easy to talk to."

"I felt the same ease with you. I shared all about my mother and my feelings for her."

"Yes, you did, and you made quite an impression on me," Mary says. "Well, awhile back my friend, one of the women I am here with this evening, told me about a medium who's really good. She communicates with the spirit world, my friend said."

I make a face. "I know, I know," Mary says. "I was skeptical, too. This medium is supposedly the real deal. So I made an appointment, having never lost the desire to speak with my dad one more time." I soften. This isn't so far from what I experienced last night. Maybe I'm a believer now. Mary continues, "Now that I see you right in front of me, Chris, I know what she said is true."

"Me? How do I play into this?"

"This might upset you," Mary says, "but here goes. My appointment was last week, and when I was with the medium, she told me things about my dad and me only my dad would know. Details like my nickname—he called me "Pumpkin" because of my chubby cheeks— and about a dinner he planned for my thirteenth birthday, just the two of us, and other things like that. But she kept saying that a woman was cutting in, trying to be heard. This woman wanted me to give a message to someone, to her son. She said I had painted a portrait of her years ago, and given it to this man, no charge. She was that man's mother."

What is she telling me?

"You are the only person I've ever gifted a portrait too, Chris. You see, this spirit said that she was your mother. She said that I would be seeing you soon and that I would need to give him a message. She said that I might not recognize you immediately, but that it would come to me.

Chris, it was your mother."

I'm stunned beyond talking.

"The medium fell into a trance and said something that makes no sense to me, so somehow I feel I have failed with this message. It was something about a river. A turn in the river, to be exact. She said you would know what that means. I'm sorry, Chris. I know this probably makes no sense."

I can't find my voice to respond. This woman has no idea just how much sense this makes to me. I just stare at her blankly.

Then she goes on. "She also said that the 'nudges' are for real, the clock and the photo. Chris, does any of this mean anything?"

"Anything?" I sputter. "It means *everything*. It's my sign."

"Chris, I can see that you need time to digest this... believe me, I'm just now coming to terms with my own experience with the medium. I believe we met twenty years ago for an important reason, for both of us, and I believe we've met again for the same. Really, there are no coincidences. So good to see you," Mary says. She touches my arm and kisses my cheek and she begins to leave. Her friends join her at the door.

I ask her quickly, "Do you still live in the same house? Can I stop by and have coffee with you one day, tell you about a dream I had?"

Mary turns back to me. "There's nothing I would love more," she answers. "Now go back and enjoy your family. Until next time..." and she gives my arm a final squeeze.

I shut my eyes and held back my tears and the world melts away. I bask in a moment of absolute peace. It's as if I'm a child and my mother holds me for one final moment. And in this moment I know for certain that I am right with the world and everything in it. I let out an audible sigh and know that I can finally, one hundred percent, let go.

"Wake up, regain your humor.
You are already free!"
— Dan Millman

I'm Chris Scalera.

I'm the son of John and Diane, both born and raised in the Bronx, New York.

I'm one of six children: three brothers and two sisters.

I was born in the suburbs of Carmel, New York.

Although I lived in a few different towns, I consider Mahopac, New York my home. As of this writing, I live there with my wife Michelle and two sons, Brandon and Chris.

I've been self-employed for most of my adult life as a home exterior remodeler. I have a showroom on the main road in my town. My current business is known as The Vinyl King. I used to be The Blind Man.

As I look back on my fiftieth birthday, I'm grateful my mother came to me, and gave me the best present ever.

She gave me the ability to jump in that river, to let go and to live on, in peace and clarity, to the river's end.

She gave me my sign.

She gave me the gift of walking back into that dining room at Mama Rosa's, among my friends and family, embracing my life in full, the whole river, with its twists and turns, opening up to its warm, calm waters.

The End

*The author and his
mother, circa 1980.*

Acknowledgments

I thank my wife Michelle and my two sons, Brandon and Christopher, whom I love very much. If I could put a special order in to God for a family, I would want exactly the one I have. I am truly blessed to live a life filled with love, and knowing they are at the end of every challenge makes it all a breeze.

Special thanks to my business partner Kevin McKenna, and his wife Teresa. When I had finished only a couple of chapters of this book, I read it to Kevin and his positive reaction inspired me to continue. He eventually brought some of my scribble home to his wife who took my long run-on sentence and made it legible. Thank you, Teresa, for being so kind and generous. Without you, my story would have died at my desk.

Thanks to all my great friends and family who are mentioned in my book who made life so much fun and so special. When I finished my book, I told my wife there is only one person whose opinion I truly value, my very, very special uncle, Brandon. If he says it's good, it's good, and if he says it's not, it's not. He's my mother's brother, and I named my firstborn after him. He's been there my entire life with love, a smile, and a book. In return, he expects my second book to be better than this one (no pressure!). Thank you, Uncle Brandon, for being a great example and inspiration. And thank you for giving my manuscript to the brilliant Chet Kozlowski...what a blessing. Chet not only shaped it and made sense of it all, he made it all way to easy for me to bring it to a finish. Thank you very much, Chet. You are truly special.

Christopher J. (Chris) Scalera lives and writes in Upstate New York with his wife and two sons. A successful, self-employed home exterior remodeler, he has no formal training in writing. The events in this book are essentially the events of his life. He strives to be spiritually centered and to inspire others. This is his first book.